아이브라운
www.ibroun.com
에서 동영상 강의 중!

이것이 논리다!

이 종 현 저

BROUNEDU
브라운 대학편입
학원에서 실강 중!

도서출판 상 학 당

There is only one thing that makes
a dream impossible to achieve
the fear of failure.

꿈을 불가능으로 만드는 데에는
단 한 가지 요소가 존재한다.
실패에 대한 두려움이다.

- Paulo Coelho -

머리말

학생들이 편입 영어를 공부하다 보면 논리 부분에서 막힌 기분이 들 때가 많습니다. 영어 구문을 공부해도 막상 빈칸 문제를 보면 빈칸에 어떤 내용을 넣어줘야 할지 감을 못잡을 때가 아주 많습니다.

이 교재는 그런 학생들을 위해 준비한 책입니다. 편입 영어 문제에서 빈칸에 알맞은 것을 넣는 논리 문제에서 빈칸에 어떤 말을 넣을지 정확한 근거를 잡고 그 근거에 맞게 답을 찍는 훈련을 할 것입니다.

모든 논리 문제의 정답은 지문 속에 있습니다. 이 책을 통해 여러분들이 문제 풀이법을 정확하게 익혀서 어떤 논리 문제를 만나도 정확하게 답을 찍고 편입에 성공하기를 소망합니다.

저자 올림

논리 문제 접근법

⁞ 논리 유형 문제를 접근하는 방법! ⁞

1. 한 두 문장의 짧은 논리 문제를 풀 때

1) 두 문장으로 나눌 것!
   ➡ 한 문장으로 된 문제라고 해도 의미 단위의 두 문장으로 쪼갤 것!

2) 같은 방향인지, 다른 방향인지 파악!
   ➡ 같은 방향이면 같은 이야기(순접), 다른 방향이면 반대 이야기(역접)

3) 역접의 연결사가 없는 이상, 이어지는 문장은 같은 내용이다.
   ➡ 모르겠으면 같은 문장을 만들어주겠다는 마음으로 접근!

4) 빈칸을 먼저 주관식으로 만들 것!(중요)

2. 여러 문장의 긴 논리 문제를 풀 때

1) 빈칸의 근거를 지문 속에서 찾는 것이 중요하다. 빈칸을 기준으로
   - 앞 뒤 문장에서 근거를 찾는다(논리성).
   - 빈칸 문장을 제외한 주제문이 될만한 표현에서 빈칸의 근거를 찾는다 (통일성).

2) 근거를 잡은 후 빈칸을 주관식으로 만들어준다(가장 중요함).

3) 주관식을 바탕으로 오답 선지 분석

- 주관식과 반대선지 : 우리가 잡은 주관식의 내용과 반대 내용으로 쓴 선지
- 관련 없는 내용 : 우리가 잡은 주관식과 아무 관련이 없는 내용의 선지
- 역추론 : 빈칸에 선지를 넣은 후 역으로 지문 속에서 근거를 찾는 것

차 례

PART. I

같은 방향

UNIT 1	인과관계
UNIT 2	재진술과 부연설명
UNIT 3	동등비교 / 유사비교 / 비유
UNIT 4	목적 / 수단
UNIT 5	예 시
UNIT 6	시간 / 조건의 부사절 / 구

UNIT 1 인과관계

1. 인과관계의 신호

원인 ⇨ 결과

1. accordingly, consequently, for this reason, therefore, hense, so, then, thus, as a result

2. cause, lead to, create, generate, affect, result in, produce, bring about, trigger, set off, touch off, stimulate, galvanize, activate

3. so ~ that s v ~, such ~ that ~
   too ~ to v
   This is why(because)
   B be followed by A

4. The result(consequence) is that ~

5. It follows that s v ~

6. be to blame for
   be responsible for ~

결과 ⇨ 원인

1. S V ~, because/as/since/now that s v ~

2. because of, owing to, due to, on account of, thanks to, by reason of, by virtue of, on the ground of

3. as a result of, in consequence of

4. in response to

5. result from, be caused by

6. 결과 reflect 원인

7. A be attributed to B
   (결과) (원인)

예시문제

1. Because she was so ________________, Mary rarely spoke in groups of people.

(A) reticent
(B) congenial
(C) brusque
(D) gregarious
(E) scurrilous

2. The villagers ________ the bandits so thoroughly that most of the survivors never picked up a weapon again without starting to cry.

(A) exuded
(B) coaxed
(C) routed
(D) swayed

3. It is no accident that most people find Davis' book disturbing, for it is ____________ to undermine a number of beliefs they have long ______________.

(A) calculated - cherished
(B) annotated - assimilated
(C) intended - denied
(D) anxious - misunderstood
(E) reputed - anticipated

4. Aptly enough, this work so imbued with the notion of changing times and styles has been constantly ______________ over the years, thereby reflecting its own mutability.

(A) appreciated
(B) emulated
(C) criticized
(D) revised
(E) reprinted

5. Because early United States writers thought that the mark of great literature was grandiosity and elegance not to be found in common speech, they ____________ the vernacular.

(A) dissected
(B) avoided
(C) misunderstood
(D) investigated
(E) exploited

6. Ironically, the proper use of figurative language must be based on the denotative meaning of the words, because it is the failure to recognize this ____________ meaning that leads to mixed metaphors and their attendant incongruity.

(A) esoteric
(B) literal
(C) latent
(D) allusive
(E) symbolic

7. Today water is more ____________ in landscape architecture than ever before, because technological advances have made it easy, in some instances even ______________, to install water features in public places.

(A) conspicuous - prohibitive
(B) sporadic - effortless
(C) indispensable - intricate
(D) ubiquitous - obligatory
(E) controversial - unnecessary

8. The struggle to earn a place on that narrow pedestal encourages people to slave away for incomparably long hours. In America the consequences of not being at the top are so dramatic that rat race is ____________. In a winner-takes-all society you would expect this time crunch.

(A) exacerbated
(B) divested
(C) stinted
(D) maligned

9. Because the high seriousness of their narratives resulted in part from their metaphysics, Southern writers were praised for their __________________ bent.

(A) technical
(B) discursive
(C) hedonistic
(D) philosophical
(E) scientific

10. The phenomenon of compulsive consumption, the fear of boredom, and the need for escape, are among the factors that in various degrees and fashions have ①__________ the growth of what is called kitsch. Kitsch is one of the most typical products of modernity. However, this alone would not be sufficient reason for discussing kitsch ②____________ the ideas of modernity, the avant-garde, and decadence, which, on the one hand, are so closely related through the ③___________ theme of time, and on the other, are so much wider in scope.

(A) ① resulted from – ② apart from – ③ dyadic
(B) ① contributed to – ② along with – ③ common
(C) ① attributed to – ② as regards – ③ linear
(D) ① coincided with – ② as to – ③ bifurcated

11. David Keith, a professor at Harvard University, has been studying how to reflect sunlight back from an artificial layer of haze in the stratosphere similar to that created by the sulfur thrown up by large volcanic eruptions, which are known to cool the Earth. One of the risks would be that such particles can encourage chemical reactions which ①__________ the ozone layer. Dr. keith and his colleagues want to study how the rates of such reactions depend on the sizes of the particles and background levels of water vapour; that would help to assess the risks and perhaps find ways to limit them. They have designed a system which would hand below a large balloon 20 km up in the sky. It would create a small ②___________ of sulfate particles and then measure the physical and chemical changes.

(A) ① deplete – ② plume
(B) ① decrease – ② abattoir
(C) ① diminish – ② cambric
(D) ① query – ② shower

12. The diplomat, selected for her demonstrated patience and skill in conducting such delicate negotiations, __________ to make a decision during the talks because any sudden commitment at that time would have been __________.

(A) resolved - detrimental
(B) refused - apropos
(C) declined - inopportune
(D) struggled - unconscionable
(E) hesitated - warranted

13. Until quite recently research on diabetes had as a kind of holding action attempted to refine the __________ of the disease primarily because no preventive strategy seemed at all likely to be __________.

(A) definition - necessary
(B) anticipation - acceptable
(C) understanding - costly
(D) treatment - practicable
(E) symptoms - feasible

14. Human nature and long distances have made exceeding the speed limit a __________ tradition in the state, so the legislators surprised no one when, acceding to public practice, they __________ increased penalties for speeding.

(A) disquieting - endorsed
(B) long-standing - considered
(C) controversial - suggested
(D) cherished - rejected
(E) hallowed - investigated

15. The National Archives contain information so __________ that researchers have been known never to publish because they cannot bear to bring their studies to an end.

(A) divisive
(B) seductive
(C) selective
(D) repetitive
(E) resourceful

16. So much of modern fiction in the United States is autobiographical, and so much of the autobiography fictionalized, that the __________ sometimes seem largely __________.

(A) authors – ignored
(B) needs – unrecognized
(C) genres – interchangeable
(D) intentions – misunderstood
(E) misapprehensions – uncorrected

17. The failure of many psychotherapists to __________ the results of pioneering research could be due in part to the specialized nature of such findings : even __________ findings may not be useful.

(A) understand – baffling
(B) envision – accessible
(C) utilize – momentous
(D) reproduce – duplicated
(E) affirm – controversial

18. This book is not destined for scholars or philosophers alone. The fundamental problems of human culture have a general human interest, and they should be made accessible to the general public. I have tried, ________, to avoid all technicalities and to express my thoughts as clearly and simply as possible. My critics should, however, be warned that what I could give here is more an explanation and illustration than a demonstration of my theory.

(A) therefore
(B) however
(C) moreover
(D) nevertheless
(E) otherwise

19. GM has apologized but has done little to address perceptions of company negligence or propose a solution so it doesn't happen again, says USC marketing professor Ira Kalb. After Toyota recalled millions of vehicles because of 'unintended acceleration,' Kalb estimates, the company lost $9 billion in sales. Since then, Toyota has recovered enough to be the best-selling automaker globally for the past two years. Because Americans typically buy cars every six years or so, GM may benefit from ____________.

(A) inflation
(B) consumer report
(C) global marketing
(D) consumer amnesia
(E) recession

20. It's hard to be a good liar, even when it comes to your own intentions, which only you can verify. Intentions come from emotions, and emotions have evolved displays on the face and body. Unless you are a master of the Stainslavsky method, you will have trouble faking them; in fact, they probably evolved because they were hard to fake. Worse, lying is stressful, and anxiety has its own telltale markers. They are the rationale for polygraphs, the so-called lie detectors, and humans evolved to be lie detectors, too. Then there is the annoying fact that some propositions logically entail others. Since some of the things you say will be true, you are always in danger of exposing your own lies. As the Yiddish saying goes, a liar must have a good ________________.

(A) memory
(B) emotion
(C) intention
(D) attitude

21. Because of its lack of theaters, the city came, ironically, to be viewed as an __________ theater town, and that reputation led entrepreneurs to believe that it would be _________ to build new theaters there.

(A) unprofitable - risky
(B) untapped - pointless
(C) unappreciated - difficult
(D) unlikely - appropriate
(E) unimpressed - shrewd

22. High-quality treatment for neuropathic pain is not consistently implemented in the medical community, because the results of scientific investigations for treatment are not currently reliable; they include strong variance in the populations studied, especially in children, which renders them ____________.

(A) justifiable
(B) synthesized
(C) incomparable
(D) interchangeable

23. The most important variables that distinguish one culture from another are not easily observable phenomena such as dress, housing, food, or table manners but rather, underlying values, attitudes, beliefs, and worldviews that shape how a culture perceives itself and others. Because these elements, which are below the level of conscious awareness, form such a large part of culture, it is difficult for people to describe their own cultural ways without _________. Just as native speakers of a language who have not studied language often have a lot of problems in explaining the grammatical structures, members of a particular culture who have not learned to study culture find it difficult to explain the components of culture and to comprehend how these shape people's perspectives and interpretations of the world.

(A) interaction
(B) training
(C) imagination
(D) acculturation

24. Some popular dishes have so many ___________ that even people within the same city cannot agree on how they whould be prepared.

(A) variations
(B) descriptions
(C) flavors
(D) critics
(E) ingredients

25. Dawkins points out that an organism differs from a rock or a river because it is inclined to ①____________. Any organism that has evolved to be violent is a member of a species whose other member, on average, have evolved to be just as violent. If you attack one of your own kind, your adversary may be as strong and pugnacious as you are, and armed with the same weapons and defenses. The likelihood that, in attacking a member of your own species, you will hurt is a powerful selection pressure that disfavors indiscriminate pouncing or lashing out. It also rules out most folk theories of violence, such as a thirst for blood, a death wish, a killer instinct, and other destructive itches, urges, and impulses. When a tendency toward violence evolves, it is always ②_____________.

(A) ① hit back - ② strategic
(B) ① get in the way - ② passive
(C) ① pursue its interests - ② lethal
(D) ① callously exploit others - ② straightforward

26. When average temperatures increase very slowly, it becomes difficult to notice the difference in baseline standards for normalcy because the shift is all but ____________.

(A) advantageous
(B) imperceptible
(C) catastrophic
(D) undeniable
(E) naturalistic

27. Mary Wollstonecraft's ______________ of female equality made her writings highly influential in the early woman's movement.

(A) election
(B) advocacy
(C) neglect
(D) suspicion
(E) detection

28. That today's students of American culture tend to ignore classical music is understandable. In our own time, America's musical high culture has degenerated into a formulaic entertainment divorced from the contemporary moment. Thus, to miss out on what our orchestras are up to is not to ______________ much. In the late Gilded Age, however, music was widely esteemed as the 'queen of the arts.' Classical music was in its American heyday, centrally embedded in the culture at large.

(A) sacrifice
(B) assume
(C) denigrate
(D) appreciate

29. The Mojave Desert's boundaries are generally ____________ by the presence of Yucca brevifolia(Joshua trees), considered and indicator species for the region.

(A) integrated
(B) demarcated
(C) standardized
(D) challenged
(E) polarized

30. Mrs. Amherst was such a sensitive and ____________ librarian that she had the ability to know exactly which book would suit each one of the students.

(A) caustic
(B) pedantic
(C) refined
(D) discerning

31. In the current economic climate, it has become popular to posit that savvy job-seekers ought to establish at least a year's worth of experience in any given position, so as to demonstrate their ____________ to future employers. Indeed, those who make this suggestion often quote each other in the media in what essentially amounts to congratulatory, self-serving articles. ____________ these so-called pundits often betray their lack of expertise by then suggesting the omission of jobs that last less than one year from a job-seeker's resume.

(A) vigor - Conversely
(B) valor - Indeed
(C) firmness - Therefore
(D) reliability - Yet

32. In order to ______________ ratings, the incumbent directed party loyalists to flood the media with __________ about recent developments in job creation.

(A) bolster - accolades
(B) improve - rumors
(C) nullify - falsehoods
(D) mollify - announcements

33. An organism's color can serve a(n) _____________ function in numerous ecological contexts, including crypsis (the ability to avoid detection), communication, and thermoregulation. As such, it is likely that organismal color reflects a balance among numerous and perhaps competing demands; a color best suited for the performance of one function(e.g., avoidance of predators) may reflect a trade-off with that suited for another(e.g, attractiveness to potential mates). This trade-off is further shaped by the wavelengths of light available in the organism's natural environment; a color pattern that is __________ in one environment may be conspicuous in another. In other words, the relative strength of the color signal depends not only on the visual system of the receiver but also on the medium and surrounding environment in which it is transmitted.

(A) unique - expedient
(B) adaptive - cryptic
(C) complicated - transient
(D) discriminant - hidden

34. Rick closed the kitchen door to keep the smell of popcorn from ______________ upstairs because he didn't want his sister to know that he was making a snack.

(A) wafting
(B) festering
(C) rending
(D) auguring

35. People become what they do. This explanation of how people acquire attitude and traits dates back to the late British philosopher Gilbert Ryle but was formalized by the social psychologist Daryl Bem in his self - perception theory. People draw inferences about who turns common wisdom on its head. People act the way they do because of their personality traits and attitudes, right? They return a lost wallet because they're honest, and recycle their trash because they care about the environment. It's evident that ______________, but Bem's insight was to suggest that the reverse also holds. If we return a lost wallet, there's an upward tick on our honesty meter. After we drag the recycling bin to the curb, we infer that we really care about the environment.

(A) character archives our most cherished ideas
(B) behavior emanates from our inner dispositions
(C) perspectives fuel the development of our perception
(D) self - motivation relies on external factors

36. I prefer to shop in a store that has a one-price policy because, whenever I ______________ with a shopkeeper, I am never certain that I paid a fair price for the articles I purchased.

(A) haggle
(B) fumble
(C) fugle
(D) ramble

37. Parasitic plants are plants that survive by using food produced by host plants rather than by producing their own food from the Sun's energy. Because they do not need sunlight to survive, parasitic plants are generally found in ____________ areas rather than in areas exposed to direct sunlight. Parasitic plants attach themselves to host plants, often to the stems or roots, by means of haustoria, which the parasite uses to make its way into the food channels of the host plant and absorb the nutrients that it needs to survive from the host plants. The world's heaviest flower, a species of rafflesia, is a parasite that lives off of the roots of jungle vines. Each of these ______________ blooms can weigh up to 15 pounds and can measure up to 3 feet across.

(A) fertile - bulky
(B) parched - exuberant
(C) alluvial - meager
(D) umbrageous - ponderous

38. Because he was ______________ in the performance of his duties, his employers could not complain about his work.

(A) derelict
(B) dilatory
(C) asinine
(D) assiduous

39. Inflation did ______________ because of government spending cuts and continued high interest rates, but the 'cure' ______________ the business recession under way since 1979, leading to the worst downturn in the economy since the 1930s. Factories closed, businesses went bankrupt, and farm mortgages were foreclosed at an increasing rate. By the end of 1982, more than 12 million Americans were out of work, more than 10 percent of the labor force. Double-digit inflation had been ended at the cost of double-digit unemployment.

(A) occur – exacerbated
(B) abate – accelerated
(C) ripple – quashed
(D) decline – appeased

40. The study of ______________ bodies has been greatly advanced by the new telescope.

(A) sidereal
(B) faunal
(C) sepulchral
(D) alluvial

41. Aristotle considers the term to be defined as a name of the essence of a thing, and the defining formula as the description of that essence. And he insists that the defining formula must give a(n) ________________ of the essence or the essential properties of the thing in question; thus a statement like 'A puppy has four legs,' although true, is not a satisfactory definition, since it does not include all features relevant with the essence of puppiness, but holds true of some, is not true of all puppies; and it describes what is not an essential but merely an accidental property of the defined term.

(A) exhaustive description
(B) major premise
(C) chained deduction
(D) inductive antithesis

42. The aye-aye of Madagascar is one of the rarest primates in the world. Its most striking feature is a very long middle finger with which it extracts burrowing insect larvae from wood and pulp from fruits. In its search for food, it taps gently on wood surfaces in order to ____________ and to assess their contents. It then bites into the soft wood with its sharp incisor teeth to open up the gallery and pokes its long finger in to extract the prize. Young aye-ayes learn at an early age from their mothers how to search for and extract insect larvae with their curious digit. They are clumsy at first, tapping everything they find, but with experience they ____________.

(A) forage feeding sites - deter predators easily
(B) locate cavities - gain dexterity rapidly
(C) scavenge with ease - flush insects skillfully
(D) regurgitate worms - scoop up the prey thoroughly

43. Counterfeiters can go to great lengths to ______________ the age of a painting, including baking it to add cracks.

(A) verify
(B) preserve
(C) invalidate
(D) fabricate

UNIT 2 재진술과 부연설명

재진술과 부연설명의 표현

in essence(fact)	in other words
namely	that is (to say)
in short(in brief)	to put it differently
in effect	to put it another way
so to speak	in simpler terms
and	to make a long story short
;	as It were
:	-ing ~/p.p ~ , s v ~
,	s v ~ , -ing ~/p.p ~
—	What is worse, ~

예 시 문 제

1. She was appalled at the mayor's policy, feeling he had ______ the promises made during his campaign.

(A) challenged
(B) exaggerated
(C) misunderstood
(D) hindered
(E) abjured

2. When Jen learned that her manager's nephew had been promoted over her, she became irate, claiming that the company practiced ______.

(A) altruism
(B) relativism
(C) malfeasance
(D) ingratitude
(E) nepotism

3. The intelligence community should not be ______ for not foreseeing the fall of the Soviet Union; even Hedrick Smith, the author of the Russians, stated in 1986 that the Soviet Union is the world's most stable society.

(A) applauded
(B) reproved
(C) espoused
(D) bolstered
(E) disavowed

4. The ___________ singer would often start a concert in a sad mood, leave halfway through in a rage, and then come back at the end as happy as can be.

(A) judicious
(B) mercurial
(C) shrewd
(D) sturdy

5. Among the successors of Hume, sanity has meant superficiality, and ____________ has meant some degree of madness.

(A) profundity
(B) delusion
(C) impunity
(D) quandary

6. ①_______________ and corruption are hollowing out the foundations of the state itself. Government ②___________ at all levels is now riddled with graft. Corruption watch, an NGO, says it has received more than 1,000 reports relating to ③__________ school principals, who have been stealing cash from their school's bank accounts.

(A) ① Malfeasance – ② pedigree – ③ uxorious
(B) ① Bribery – ② spending – ③ precocious
(C) ① Fraud – ② oversight – ③ frolicsome
(D) ① Cronyism – ② procurement – ③ crooked

7. Hammerhead sharks are the most negatively buoyant and also have very small mouths proportionally __________.

(A) to other species
(B) to those of other species
(C) to that of other species
(D) to the species

8. The phrase 'suppressed on political grounds' casts a shadow of a ______________ government blocking its citizens from receiving information that it perceives to be embarrassing or threatening.

(A) heavy-handed
(B) big-boned
(C) brown-eyed
(D) mealy-mouthed

9. Today we are immersed in memes. They spread by imitation and natural ①______________, exploiting the receptivity of the human mind to new information and influence, forged in childhood. Uncritical copying is favored. People just can't help picking stuff up, ②______________.

(A) ① credulity — ② willy-nilly
(B) ① perspicacity — ② fastidiously
(C) ① intractability — ② truculently
(D) ① fecundity — ② tremulously

10. It is widely believed that infant experience establishes certain patterns and sets forces in motion and that during the remainder of childhood, the child must deal with the ____________ of these early features.

(A) catharsis
(B) upshot
(C) derision
(D) opalescence

11. Smartwatches' abilities to pay for our food and monitor our physical activities are only possible thanks to the myriad sensors packed into their tiny metal bodies.
These sophisticated sensors, however, are gradually chipping away your digital ①____________. The basic principal behind this side effect is similar to the way in which intelligent keystroke-tracking programs have been shown to be able to recognize individual people based on behavioral biometrics profiles created from their typing habits. A hand's movement through space, while slightly different from person to person, could, in theory, be mined for personal credentials and used to make smarter attempts at compromising someone's logins. ②____________, the size of most keyboards and pin pads are standardized to make people feel more comfortable while using them.

(A) ① identity – ② As a result
(B) ① existence – ② In other words
(C) ① status – ② On the contrary
(D) ① privacy – ② What is worse

12. The earliest Western theory of art proposed that art was mimesis, __________ of reality.

(A) calumny
(B) caveat
(C) tumescence
(D) semblance

13. One virus strain that may help gene therapists cure genetic brain diseases can enter the peripheral nervous system and travel to the brain, ____________ the need to inject the therapeutic virus directly into the brain.

(A) suggesting
(B) intensifying
(C) elucidating
(D) satisfying
(E) obviating

14. Yet as Wilson suggests, our ①____________ insistence on free agency makes a kind of evolutionary sense. Indeed, humanity's ②__________ evolutionary advantage has been its drive to create collective meaning. That drive is as ingenious as it is relentless, and it can find a way to make sense of despair, depression, catastrophe, genocide, war, disaster, plagues and even the humiliations of science.

(A) ① indefatigable — ② myopic
(B) ① dogged — ② keenest
(C) ① tepid — ② peevish
(D) ① minuscule — ② tenacious

15. The reindeer live free apart until they are ①__________ from the tundra into a huge enclosure. The herders and other owners stand watching them for hours, occasionally pulling one out with a lasso. Reindeer are marked by patterns of notches cut into their ears, unique to every owner: herders have a(n) ②__________ ability to see a mark from a distance on a fast-moving creature. I stand in the fence, mesmerized by the thousands of beasts circling the muddy enclosure, a blur of antlers, mud and hooves.

(A) ① wrangled — ② uncanny
(B) ① gathered — ② chauvinist
(C) ① adumbrated — ② preternatural
(D) ① culled — ② desultory

16. In the drama playing out across North Africa and the Middle East, Morocco is going somewhat off script. While tens of thousands marched nationwide, denouncing corruption and demanding democratic reform, few called for the ousting of the nation's ruler, King Mohammad VI. The monarch is a(n) __________ figure, credited with bringing stability and prosperity to the country.

(A) incompetent
(B) irresponsible
(C) popular
(D) indifferent
(E) tyrannical

17. The natures of social history and lyric poetry are ①__________, social history always recounting the ②__________ and lyric poetry speaking for unchanging human nature, timeless essence beyond fashion and economics.

(A) ① predetermined - ② bygone
(B) ① antithetical - ② evanescent
(C) ① interdependent - ② unnoticed
(D) ① irreconcilable - ② unalterable
(E) ① indistinguishable - ② transitory

18. Originally, most intellectual criticism of mass culture was ①________ in character, being based on the assumption that the wider the appeal, the more ②________ the product.

(A) ①unpredictable - ② undesirable
(B) ① ironic - ② popular
(C) ① extreme - ② outlandish
(D) ① frivolous - ② superfluous
(E) ① negative - ② shoddy

19. When a drone looks at a thing, that thing has a way of looking like a target. People become silhouettes at a shooting range. Buildings look vulnerable, their roofs helplessly exposed and defenseless. Most colors disappear, and the remaining blacks, whites and greys evacuate the scene of all human meaning. What we see becomes ____________: body counts, damage reports, strategic value.

(A) reality
(B) nothing
(C) illusion
(D) chaos
(E) date

20. Future generations will probably consider current speculations about humanity's place in the universe to be ________________ omissions and errors: even rigorous scientific views change sometimes overnight.

(A) immune from
(B) marred by
(C) uncorrupted by
(D) correct despite
(E) abridged by

21. Unenlightened authoritarian managers rarely recognize a crucial reason for the low levels of serious conflict among members of democratically run work groups: a modicum of tolerance for dissent often prevents ___________.

(A) demur
(B) schism
(C) cooperation
(D) compliance
(E) shortsightedness

22. Marshall's confrontational style could alienate almost anyone: he even antagonized a board of directors that included a number of his supporters and that had a reputation for not being easily ________________.

(A) intimidated
(B) mollified
(C) reconciled
(D) provoked
(E) motivated

23. Word order in a sentence was much freer in Old French than it is in French today; this ____________ disappeared as the French language gradually lost its case distinctions.

(A) restriction
(B) license
(C) similarity
(D) rigidity
(E) imperative

24. ____________ matters. Losing the right to drive is, for many elderly people, as traumatic as being widowed. And, as the population ages, that trauma will be felt by more and more people in the future. Yet the safety of other road users, let alone that of an elderly driver himself, is paramount.

(A) Spouse
(B) Money
(C) Mobility
(D) Friendship
(E) Longevity

25. Robin's words were not without emotion: they retained their level tone only by a careful ____________ imminent extremes.

(A) equipoise between
(B) embrace of
(C) oscillation between
(D) limitation to
(E) subjection to

26. Mac Rory's conversation was __________: she could never tell a story, chiefly because she always forgot it, and she was never guilty of a witticism, unless by accident.

(A) scintillating
(B) unambiguous
(C) perspicuous
(D) stultifying
(E) facetious

27. The pungent verbal give-and-take among the characters makes the novel ①______________ reading, and this very ②______________ suggests to me that some of the opinions voiced may be the author's.

(A) ① disturbing - ② flatness
(B) ① tedious - ② inactiveness
(C) ① lively - ② spiritedness
(D) ① necessary - ② steadiness
(E) ① rewarding - ② frivolousness

28. The ①______________ of gamblers' unsuccessful decision strategies is one ②__________ of the illusions built into games of chance in order to misguide players and take their money.

(A) ① distortion - ② outcome
(B) ① restriction - ② result
(C) ① maintenance - ② function
(D) ① prediction - ② accomplishment
(E) ① demonstration - ② prerequisite

29. For decades, the concept of supersymmetry has been one of the biggest ①______________ in modern physics, having repeatedly ②__________ scientists' attempts at understanding.

(A) ①enigmas - ② confirmed
(B) ① theorems - ② subdued
(C) ① conundrums - ② stymied
(D) ① hypotheses - ② obscured
(E) ① predicaments - ② foretold

30. Some critics have suggested that the author's study of anthropology ①____________ his literary style, and indeed, anthropological references often ②___________ his works.

(A) ① influenced - ② maintain
(B) ① demeaned - ② pervade
(C) ① informed - ② pepper
(D) ① challenged - ② fill
(E) ① determined - ② coddle

31. Standing aloof from academic squabbles, the writer is able to discuss complex debates in a clear and ①____________ manner that is remarkably free of insider ②______________.

(A) ① ingenuous - ② euphemism
(B) ① unequivocal - ② admonition
(C) ① supercilious - ② contingency
(D) ① lucid - ② jargon
(E) ① precise - ② alacrity

32. The quest for absolute zero, the lowest temperature theoretically possible, has become, for some scientists, ______________ to the search for the Holy Grail.

(A) cognate
(B) analogous
(C) conducive
(D) subordinate

33. The sagacious student of literature is aware that terms used in literary criticism are ______________ in that their meanings shift depending on the premises of the writer using them and the nature of the work under discussion.

(A) typically inert
(B) totally infeasible
(C) notoriously plastic
(D) completely arbitrary

34. The majority of the villagers in this seemingly forgotten land are __________ vegetarians; that is, they only eat meat during a holy celebration, or whenever they can afford it, which because of the ludicrously high prices, is practically never.

(A) reluctant
(B) strict
(C) staunch
(D) clandestine

35. The phrase 'catch-22' originated in Joseph Heller's novel Catch-22, in which a soldier asks to be relieved from combat and is given the __________ explanation that the criterion for being relieved of duty is being insane, and that since he is asking not to be involved in the insanity of war he must be sane, and therefore cannot be relieved based on insanity.

(A) cursory
(B) plausible
(C) convoluted
(D) parsimonious

36. Pathfinding in games must appeal to player expectations for plausibility and naturalness, that is, what natural intelligence might conceivably do. Thus, navigation in games is not necessarily optimal for maximum machine efficiency or for shortest distance. Indeed, these goals are assumed to be secondary and possibly even undesirable. That is, if they lead to unrealistic, mechanical-looking movement lacking in sensori-emotional or aesthetic qualities, movement as such __________ players and detracts from the game's replay appeal and immersive quality.

(A) stimulates
(B) degrades
(C) disconcerts
(D) dehumanizes

37. Marx's ___________ that "men make their own history, but not in conditions of their own making" has become an oft-repeated dictum.

(A) admonition
(B) aphorism
(C) euphoria
(D) apprehension
(E) prefiguration

38. What creates tension in a piece of fiction is partly the way the concrete words are linked together to make up the visible action of the story. But it's also the things that are ①___________, that are implied, the landscape just ②___________ the smooth surface of things.

(A) ① illuminated - ② on
(B) ① curtailed - ② across
(C) ① marked down - ② at
(D) ① left out - ② under
(E) ① included - ② beside

39. Her ___________ personality was a welcome addition to the gloomy atmosphere at the annual meeting.

(A) amiable
(B) plangent
(C) lackadaisical
(D) cadaverous

40. The origins of the magnetic compass are ①__________ in mystery. No one knows who discovered the magnetic property of the lodestone. Nor anyone know who discovered that the stone's attractive power could be ②__________ to steel or hardened iron, or that the magnet could be used in determining geographic directions. The Chinese may have been the first, as early as the eleventh century, to use a magnetic needle for indicating direction.

(A) ① integrated - ② impelled
(B) ① shrouded - ② imparted
(C) ① hidden - ② bogged
(D) ① wreathed - ② marred
(E) ① expounded - ② lured

41. Diversity is often ①__________ as highly desirable. Indeed, in professional contexts, we know that more diverse teams often outperform ②__________ teams.

(A) ① touted - ② homogeneous
(B) ① extolled - ② idiosyncratic
(C) ① elevated - ② heterogeneous
(D) ① lauded - ② divisive
(E) ① adulated - ② miscellaneous

42. In the 1860s, author Leo Tolstoy was __________ with his family in the Tula region of Russia; while comfortably established there, he wrote War and Peace.

(A) castigated
(B) ensconced
(C) coerced
(D) excoriated

43. It was obvious from the concerned look at David's face that his spendthrift habits had placed him in a _________ financial situation.

(A) bumptious
(B) precarious
(C) recherche
(D) facile

44. Other comparisons carried out in the study suggest that even when Lucy walked upright, she may have done so less efficiently than modern humans, ①__________ her ability to walk long distances on the ground. In addition, all of her limb bones were found to be very strong relative to her body size, indicating that she had exceptionally strong muscles, more like those of modern chimpanzees than modern humans. ②____________ in muscle power later in human evolution may be linked to better technology that reduced the need for physical exertions and the increased metabolic demands of a larger brain.

(A) ① enhancing - ② An increase
(B) ① reflecting - ② A deterioration
(C) ① limiting - ② A reduction
(D) ① attenuating - ② A boost

45. Carver kept detailed records so that others could duplicate his experiments: he was a thorough, _________ scientist who depended more on careful experimentation than on instinct.

(A) mordant
(B) meretricious
(C) supercilious
(D) scrupulous

46. Many online consumers are __________ about leaving any footprints in cyberspace; they would quit a Web page rather than reveal any personal information about themselves.

(A) nonchalant
(B) skittish
(C) insouciant
(D) ardent

47. Garden spiders use a special silk that makes their intricate decorations __________, and experiments have shown that the decorated parts attract more insects.

(A) run off
(B) hole up
(C) stand out
(D) lay in

48. He reeled and swayed, __________ like a drunken man to keep from falling.

(A) goading
(B) primping
(C) evanishing
(D) doddering

49. It was difficult to imagine Matthew, a __________ man, as a psychiatrist; listening while others talked was not his style.

(A) heedful
(B) pessimistic
(C) tubbish
(D) voluble

50. We regard this unwarranted attack on a neutral nation as an act of ________ and we demand that it cease at once and that proper restitution be made.

(A) spoliation
(B) interstices
(C) reparation
(D) detonation

51. The public administrator to whom I have referred was most ________; he refused to accept bribe and scrutinizingly reviewed every document for preventing customers from facing predicaments.

(A) conscientious
(B) complementary
(C) puerile
(D) ignominious

52. As his ________ accelerated, he dealt his political rivalry a series of blows insidiously and then succeeded in taking the throne, trying to hold it.

(A) madrigal
(B) machination
(C) tautology
(D) subjection

53. Much of his past was unearthed, indeed, and all ①__________; tales came out of the man's cruelty, at once so callous and violent; of his ②__________ life, of his strange associates, of the hatred that seemed to have surrounded his career; but of his present whereabouts, not a whisper.

(A) ① distrustful – ② virtuous
(B) ① disreputable – ② vile
(C) ① famous – ② tough
(D) ① disrespectful – ② gentle

54. With a trusted Pygmy tracker, he would follow one group of gorillas discreetly but persistently for all of one day or several, holding back at distance enough to leave them unaware of his presence. Such ①__________ tracking allowed him to learn what they had been eating, how mony nests they had built, and how to make deductions about group size, ages, gender, while ②__________ the chance that he'd spook these very shy primates.

(A) ① fastidious – ② minimizing
(B) ① obscure – ② augmenting
(C) ① sinuous – ② abating
(D) ① eclectic – ② maintaining

55. When the parties could not reach a consensus, a labor specialist was asked to __________ in the dispute between workers and management.

(A) eradicate
(B) speculate
(C) elaborate
(D) arbitrate

UNIT 3 동등비교/유사비교/비유

동등비교/유사비교/비유의 표현

Similarly	In the same way
Likewise	By the same token
A be like B	just as S V
A is no more B than C is D	think of(regard/see/view/look upon)
as ~ as	A as B
be similar to	A is to B what C is to D
be akin to	be comparable to
be a kind of	put one in mind of
be likened to	as though(if)
is not unlike	be the same as
may be seen as	is not dissimilar to

예 시 문 제

1. There's a common notion that losing your temper must be bad for your heart. In a study carried out at the University of North Carolina in 2000, 13,000 patients were given questionnaires in which they rated their own tendency to get angry, and were followed up a few years later. Although their blood pressure was apparently normal, those who had said they frequently get angry were three times more likely to have had heart attacks in the intervening years than the others, even when factors like smoking diabetes and weight had been taken into account. ______________, Mark McDermott from the University of East London found that people who expressed their anger suffered more from heart disease than who held back from shouting.

(A) On the other hand
(B) By the way
(C) Instead
(D) In short
(E) Likewise

2. Journeys are the midwives of ____________. Few places are more conducive to internal conversations than moving planes, ships or trains.

(A) change
(B) thought
(C) reality
(D) literature

3. Processing a TV message is much more like the all-at-once processing of the ear than the linear processing of the eye reading a printed page. According to McLuhan, television is fundamentally ______________.

(A) an acoustic medium
(B) an visual medium
(C) an complementary dvice
(D) an explosive device

UNIT 4 목적/수단

목적/수단의 표현

take steps/actions/measures	The problem(trouble, difficulty) is ~
To V ~, S V ~	The dilemma(puzzle) is ~
On answer(solution resolution) ~	(only) by ~ing
As a result (of)	so that ~(in order to ~)
	(only) through

예 시 문 제

1. By __________ scientific rigor with a quantitative approach, researchers in the social sciences may often have ________ their scope to those narrowly circumscribed topics that are well-suited to quantitative methods.

(A) undermining - diminished
(B) equating - enlarged
(C) vitiating - expanded
(D) identifying - limited
(E) imbuing - broadened

2. In the drudgery of the everyday, it can be easy to become lost in boredom and self-pity. Yet some people seem remarkably resilient to life's blows: exuding the cheeriness of Mary Poppins on even the gloomiest day. How do they manage it? While some people may be blessed with a sunny temperament, there are some tried and tested ways that should help anyone to ____________. Often the techniques take just minutes to practise, yet can have lasting benefits for your general life satisfaction and well-being.

(A) beat the blues
(B) suppress the desire
(C) dwell on the pains
(D) train a good skill
(E) break through the difficulties

3. The tasks involving modern architecture and the problems it must solve are not purely connected with new additions to ancient buildings. One of the most important problems is that of modernization, and this operation logically means the use of modern architecture. The question is, exactly how far, where alterations in the internal structure of ancient buildings are required in order to ensure their survival without ________ those very qualities which make them worth preserving, is it necessary and permissible to make use of modern architectural devices?

(A) destroying
(B) accusing
(C) connecting
(D) sustaining

4. At the most basic level, language is merely a set of shared symbols or signs that a cooperative group of people has mutually agreed to use to create meaning. The relationship between the selected sign and the agreed meaning is quite ____________. We can easily illustrate this concept by looking at some of the varied symbols used by different cultures to identify a familiar household pet. In Finland, they have settled on *kissa*, but in Germany, *katze* has been chosen, while Swahili speakers use *pake*. As you can see, none of the words has any relation to the actual characteristics of a cat.

(A) close
(B) arbitrary
(C) historical
(D) ethnocentric

5. Nineteenth-century apologists for capitalism provided a rationalization for the exploitation of the poor by the rich by __________ the free market and the struggle for existence described by Darwin, in which the fit survive.

(A) transcending the kernel of
(B) contrasting the relationship between
(C) critiquing the whole idea of
(D) drawing an analogy between

6. The impressionists painted every scenes from the world we know rather than following traditional religious, historical, or mythological subjects. They painted real life landscapes as they saw them and without idealization. They were not concerned with a(n) __________ finish and applied their paint with quick, spontaneous brushstrokes. In their attempts to capture the __________ moment and the ways in which objects reflect or absorb light, Monet, Renoir, Manet, Pissarro, and others have created a new and brilliantly vivacious world on canvas; they have also influenced the work of their friends, most notably Cezanne, Degas, and Van Gogh.

(A) unsullied - immutable
(B) sloppy - temporary
(C) meticulous - fleeting
(D) unwilling - exciting
(E) succinct - unforgettable

7. By forcing our surrender to the authority of the clock, systematic timekeeping has imposed a form of __________.

(A) anarchy
(B) permanence
(C) provincialism
(D) tyranny
(E) autonomy

8. The police drove the children around in squad cars, let them talk to each other over the radios, and __________ the day by giving them ice cream.

(A) blew up
(B) wound up
(C) turned up
(D) looked up

UNIT 5 예 시

예시의 표현

For example	Examples of
For instance	Instances of
show	Shown by
An example of this	Cases of
illustrates	As an example
Illustrations of	exemplified by
Such as	llustrated by
like	seen in
especially(particularly)	in particular

예 시 문 제

1. Numerous historical examples illustrate both the overriding influence that scientists' __________ have on their interpretation of data and the consequent ___________ of their intellectual objectivity.

(A) prejudices - impairment
(B) instruments - abandonment
(C) theories - independence
(D) conclusions - coloration
(E) suppositions - reinforcement

2. A dog bone found at an Stone Age tomb in the Boyne Valley has helped to shed new light on ______________ of pet dogs. The dog bone, believed to date back almost 5,000 years, was unearthed at Newgrange in County Meath - an ancient monument built by Stone Age farmers. Scientists at Trinity College Dublin used it to sequence the dog's genome. The research suggests that modern dogs may have emerged from two separate domestications of wolves, on opposite ends of the Eurasian continent. It challenges previous theories that man's best friend originated from a single domestication of wolves in Asia.

(A) the imaginary pedigree myth
(B) the possible dual origins
(C) the hereditary consistency
(D) the genetic substance
(E) the diverse geographical distribution

3. The ancient Romans had a saying: "__________________." Every time you learn a new, useful word or phrase – be it while speaking with someone, watching a movie, or reading a book – make sure that you store the information on your phone or a notebook you keep in your pocket. This way you can review your recorded information whenever you have a free moment.

(A) Spoken words fly away, but written words stay
(B) There is something to learn from poverty
(C) A fish on the hook is better than ten in the brook
(D) Great barkers are no biters
(E) A tale grows better in the telling

4. The world is becoming __________ to tax dodgers. That is the conclusion of the latest Financial Secrecy Index. It looks at various measures of financial transparency and information-sharing in more than 90 countries, then weights them according to the level of financial services each country provides to non-residents. Most countries' scores have fallen since 2013, indicating greater transparency. Among the biggest improvers are Cayman Islands, once a notorious tax haven, and Luxembourg, which tax campaigners used to call Europe's "death star" of financial secrecy.

(A) more adjusted
(B) more used
(C) a great chance
(D) less welcoming
(E) a mega heaven

5. ______________; even within an individual patient, tumors may change over time. And doctors are learning that a melanoma growth might have more in common with a lung cancer or a brain cancer than another melanoma. "We are moving away from the concept that all lung cancers are the same and all breast cancers are the same and all colon cancers are the same," says Dr. David Solit, director of the Kravis Center for Molecular Oncology at MSKCC.

(A) Hospitals should give every cancer patient equal care
(B) Tumors come back even after treatment
(C) No two cancers are alike
(D) All cancers are fundamentally the same
(E) Cancers cannot be cured

6. Some Chinese euphemisms also stem from squeamishness. Rather than inquire about a patient's sex life, doctors may ask if you have much time for fang *shi*(room business). Online sites sell *qingqu yougpin*, literally 'interesting love products.' But Chinese circumlocution is often a form of polite opacity. Chinese people don't like being too direct in turning down invitations or (as many journalists find) requests for interviews. So they will frequently reply that something is *bu fangbian*(not conveninet). This does not mean reapply in a few weeks' time. It means ______________.

(A) they do not want to do it, ever
(B) they will do it as soon as possible
(C) they are not sure
(D) they expect you to be less ambiguous
(E) they want you to be less ambiguous

7. Often at night I dream that I've found some dangerous object lying on the floor and swallowed it. I sit up, coughing violently, trying to force it back out. I turn to my wife and tell her that I've ingested something potentially fatal, and what should I do? If she wakes up grouchy, she snaps, "Be quiet! I'm trying to sleep!" Startled, I recover myself, realize it's just the same ___________ I always have, and feel embarrassed, hoping my wife won't remember the interruption the next morning.

(A) spasm
(B) memory
(C) illustration
(D) fantasy
(E) nightmare

8. Passion and desire, their prolongation and exhaustion, may actually be Aciman's great authorial preoccupation. Life is lived at the edge of desire, in the thrill of the chase. In the essays the desire is disembodied, which in many ways makes it that much more intense. The thing about Aciman's ruminations on loss is that he does not strive to regain anything. He does not want to. It's often too obvious to be noted, but __________ of desire is its death. As Aciman says, "When you have total plenitude, you don't know what to open the door and I have a beach. But when I go to the beach, I'm always disappointed because it's boring. What do you do at a beach? There's nothing to do. But to think about going to the beach feeds me."

(A) failure
(B) reproduction
(C) displacement
(D) consummation

9. According to one survey, about one-third of all teens send more than 100 text messages a day. Some worry that teens could become addicted to this way of communication. For one teen, texting is as automatic as breathing. Doctors say that the instant ____________ of getting a text message stimulates the brain's pleasure center. Neurological research has shown that texting teens have brain scans similar to those of heroine addicts.

(A) specification
(B) apparition
(C) gratification
(D) verification
(E) specification

10. Some words used in ordinary conversation take on a specialized meaning within the context of a particular subject. In biology, ______________, the word 'producers' is not used to refer to the people who back Hollywood movies or Broadway plays. In the context of a biology textbook, 'producers' refers to a category of organisms, or living things, that acquire energy and raw materials from environmental sources and make their own food. ______________, the word 'consumers' in the context of biology doesn't refer to shoppers. It refers to organisms that cannot produce their own food and must feed off the tissue and waste of other organisms. Ordinary words that take on a specialized meaning when appearing in textbooks are just as important as those specialized vocabulary words that almost never pop up in ordinary speech.

(A) however - Thus
(B) therefore - In addition
(C) for example - Similarly
(D) for instance - As a result

11. The burqa, like some other forms of 'cover' has, in many settings, marked the symbolic separation of men's and women's spheres, as part of the general association of women with family and home, not with public space where strangers mingled. Twenty tears ago the anthropologist Hanna Papanek, who worked in Pakistan, described the burqa as ______________. She noted that many saw it as a liberating invention because it enabled women to move out of segregated living spaces while still observing the basic moral requirements of separating and protecting women from unrelated men. Such veiling signifies belonging to a particular community and participating in a moral way of life in which families are paramount in the organization of communities and the home is associated with the sanctity of women.

(A) portable seclusion
(B) camouflage for women
(C) self-defeating separatism
(D) an assertion of femininity

12. Few species illustrate the principle of '______________' as well as the salmon. The sushi staple is born in rivers, migrates to the sea once mature, then attempts a daunting run back to its birthplace to spawn the next generation. A large percentage never make it, ensuring that only those in top condition are able to pass in their genes.

(A) first come, first served
(B) survival of the fittest
(C) know thyself
(D) endure to the last
(E) better late than never

13. Today laws govern the number of hours that young people may work as well as the conditions in which they work. This was not always so, however. For example, until the twentieth century, the children of poor families in England were often exploited for inexpensive labor. This exploitation took a number of forms. Children as young as nine years old were forced to work for fourteen to sixteen hours a day. Poor working conditions seriously impaired the children's health.
Although many parents tried to envelop their children with protection and care, the families needed the money and could not fight the factory and mine owners. Many children must have felt ________________. English writers criticized such mistreatment of children. For example, Charles Dickens, the famous novelist, often described the ______________ waste of young lives.

(A) pampered - brutal
(B) forsaken - inhumane
(C) redeemed - critical
(D) abandoned - insipid

UNIT 6 시간/조건의 부사절/구

시간/조건의 부사절/구의 표현

If S V ~	Given 명/s v ~
provided s v ~	considering 명/s v ~
providing s v ~	in view of ~
supposing s v ~	when s v ~
in case s v ~	only when s v ~
only if s v ~	after 명/s v ~
If it were not for/If it had not been for	not until 명/s v ~
were it not for/had it not been for	only after 명/s v ~
without/but for	

예 시 문 제

1. Given the gravity of the situation, Terrence's __________ quips were inappropriate; he did not seem to realize it was not the time or place for sarcasm.

(A) supercilious
(B) coarse
(C) sardonic
(D) fatuous
(E) ribald

2. When people make up new words using existing words and word-forming elements, we understand them with ease providing we know what the elements they use to form those words mean and providing the word-forming rules that they ________________ are familiar.

(A) employ
(B) redact
(C) transplant
(D) clone

3. After watching the entire basketball season without ever leaving his house, he realized that his leg muscles had begun to ________________.

(A) infuse
(B) atrophy
(C) whet
(D) lug

4. Without the political will to implement them, such ambitious plans are often ______________.

(A) auspicious
(B) expeditious
(C) propitious
(D) forlorn

5. If all of Cuba's remaining stars were to hit the market at once, ______________ clubs likes the New York Yankees would once again be able to spend their way to the top of the standings.

(A) adnominal
(B) errant
(C) georgic
(D) plutocratic

6. The recent decline is largely due to oil. Considering the havoc the price drop has ①____________, most notably on Russia, Ms. Yellen was remarkably ②____________.
It would, she was confident, be a net positive for growth since America is a net oil importer. Russia's trade and financial linkages to America were minimal. Experience, she noted, suggests the impact on inflation will be ③____________.

(A) ① produced – ② optimistic – ③ unremitting
(B) ① wrought – ② sanguine – ③ transitory
(C) ① inflicted – ② upbeat – ③ sardonic
(D) ① created – ② sallow – ③ unpredictable

7. Individual freedom of thought should be ①____________ more absolutely than individual freedom of action, given that the latter, though also desirable, must be ②____________ the limits imposed by the rights and freedom of others.

(A) ① protected - ② subject to
(B) ① assessed - ② measured by
(C) ① valued - ② superior to
(D) ① exercised - ② indifferent to
(E) ① curtailed - ② conscious of

8. If the state government's latest budget problems were ①________________, it would not be useful to employ them as ②________________ examples in the effort to avoid the inevitable effects of shortsighted fiscal planning in the future.

(A) ① typical - ② representative
(B) ① exceptional - ② aberrant
(C) ① anomalous - ② illuminating
(D) ① predictable - ② helpful
(E) ① solvable - ② insignificant

9. If efficacious new medicines have side effects that are commonly observed and ①______________, such medicines are too often considered ②______________, even when laboratory tests suggest caution.

(A) ① unremarkable - ② safe
(B) ① unpredictable - ② reliable
(C) ① frequent - ② outdated
(D) ① salutary - ② experimental
(E) ① complicated - ② useful

10. Surprisingly, given the dearth of rain that fell on the corn crop, the yield of the harvest was ①___________; consequently, the corn reserves of the country have not been ②___________.

(A) ① inadequate - ② replenished
(B) ① encouraging - ② depleted
(C) ① compromised - ② salvaged
(D) ① abundant - ② extended
(E) ① disappointing - ② harmed

11. He felt it would be ①____________, in view of the intense ② ___________ that would likely follow, to make the sacrifice required in order to gain such little advantage.

(A) ① charitable - ② growth
(B) ① welcomed - ② prejudice
(C) ① futile - ② encouragement
(D) ① academic - ② acclaim
(E) ① unrealistic - ② turmoil

12. Given that he came to the mediation with such an ①___________ attitude, it is no wonder there was little movement toward any harmonious agreement; I mean, he was absolutely ②___________.

(A) ① exemplary - ② disciplined
(B) ① ingratiating - ② fixated
(C) ① immovable - ② outspoken
(D) ① obdurate - ② incorrigible

PART. II

다른 방향

UNIT 1	비교 / 대조
UNIT 2	역 접
UNIT 3	시간을 이용한 대조

UNIT 1 비교/대조

비교/대조의 표현

although(though, even though(if)) ~	alternatively
conversely	as opposed to
for all that	on the other hand
on the contrary	whereas
all the same	while
that is not the case	compared with
unlike	otherwise
different from	on the one hand ... on the other hand
opposite	by way of contrast
In comparison	It might be better if ~
An/The alternative is ~	belie
However, but	er than
Not so much A as B	rather than
= Not so much A, but B	Not A, but B
= Not so much A, rather B	far from ~
= Not A so much as B	let alone ~
= More B than A, less A than B	be challenged by
from A to B0	dilemma

예시문제

1. Our highly ____________ vocabulary for street crime contrasts sharply with our ____________ vocabulary of corporate crime, a fact that corresponds to the general public's unawareness of the extent of corporate crime.

(A) nuanced - subtle
(B) uninformative - misleading
(C) euphemistic - abstract
(D) differentiated - limited
(E) technical - jargon-laden

2. Whereas biologists must maintain a ____________ attitude toward the subjects of their research, social scientists must, paradoxically, combine personal involvement and scholarly ____________.

(A) scrupulous - sympathy
(B) careful - abandon
(C) casual - precision
(D) passive - passion
(E) disinterested - detachment

3. While many people utilize homeopathic remedies to treat health problems, other people do not ____________ such alternative treatments, ____________ conventional medical treatments instead.

(A) distrust - employing
(B) embrace - eschewing
(C) reject - envisioning
(D) countenance - relying on
(E) recommend - turning from

4. Those in favor of stronger laws to __________ gun violence mostly support the cause by arguing against the claims of the gun lobby. For gun law advocates, the case for action is overwhelming, but there's no chance of convincing the __________ minority who are so personally (or financially) invested in gun ownership.

(A) escalate – obstinate
(B) deprave – pliable
(C) dock – malleable
(D) abate – entrenched

5. Rooted in romanticism and derived from the idea of natural human rights, European laws have mostly sought to protect creators. America's notion of copyright, __________, sees culture more as a commodity. The constitution of the United states frames copyright as a reward that is granted to authors for a limited time to encourage them to be creative. __________ recently America has followed Europe's lead in extending the term of copyright to 70 years after a creator's death – not so much in belated recognition of authors' rights as in a concession to Hollywood and other important rights-holders, which had lobbled for the changes. In 1998 Dlsney and other studios even pushed through legislation that extended the copyright on films to 95 years; it became known as the "Mickey Mouse Bill".

(A) however – Consequently
(B) similarly – Nevertheless
(C) on the other hand – Yet
(D) therefore – As a result

6. In 1985 and 1986 an epidemic of asthma hit Barcelona. The city's researchers first turned to the usual suspects, such as air pollution, pollen and mould. But a series of telephone interviews with the sufferers pointed to a much more precise cause. All the attacks had occurred by the harbor, and at times when ships were unloading soya beans. The cause was clear: soya-bean dust. So was the solution: the installation of filters on the harbor's silos. Asthma is one of the world's most common chronic diseases. It affects about 300million people. Yet what triggers any given asthma attack is unclear and, as a consequence, most asthmatics are not properly treated. Stories of ____________, like that of Barcelona, are rare.

(A) total failure
(B) tragedy
(C) global scale
(D) success
(E) fatal attack

7. Old workers have traditionally earned more, reflecting the weight of seniority in pay scales, so the cost of providing final-salary pension benefits for them has been higher. In America, where employers are expected to provide health care, older workers are also more expensive to insure. On the other hand, such workers may be more flexible on pay, particularly if employers are willing to offer part-time work, which many older people prefer. That might make them ____________.

(A) more difficult to work
(B) less eligible to apply
(C) more likely to get fired
(D) less amenable to get a job
(E) more attractive to hire

8. When the world learned about the death of Cecil the Lion, a beloved resident of a national park in Zimbabwe who had been lured away by hunters, then killed and beheaded for a trophy, outrage came swiftly. Walter James Palmer, the Minnesota dentist who killed Cecil, became the target of online death threats. Investigations have been launched on two continents. But while Cecil's death has put a new focus on illegal poaching, other hunters are pursuing their own trophies — and ______________. That's because of another, less publicized side of big-game trophy hunting: the sanctioned stalking of animals that are bred, grown and kept in captivity specifically so that the right to kill them can be sold to wealthy sportsmen. It's called 'canned hunting.'

(A) it is absolutely dramatic
(B) it is perfectly legal
(C) it is less expensive
(D) it is very popular
(E) it is more humane

9. Belying his earlier reputation for ___________ as a negotiator, Morgan had recently assumed a more ___________ stance for which many of his erstwhile critics praised him.

(A) intransigence - conciliatory
(B) impropriety - intolerant
(C) inflexibility - unreasonable
(D) success - authoritative
(E) incompetence - combative

10. For some types of public figures walking away from source of their fame, the question of what comes next may be treated lightly. A retired athlete can become a sportscaster or investor; the TV actor whose hit show comes to an end can mull over movie scripts. But when a writer retires, it feels, somehow, different: writing novels is less a job one can leave than proof that one ________. There's something that seems illogical about a writer declaring he or she is done. Where, then, do all of the observations channeled into metaphor go?

(A) is sensitive and sympathetic
(B) is not interested in making money
(C) behaviors in mysterious ways
(D) spends the most time on reading
(E) sees the world in a certain way

11. Most plant species exhibit ________ in their geographical distribution: often a given species is found over a large geographical area, but individual populations within that range are widely ________.

(A) discontinuity - separated
(B) density - dispersed
(C) symmetry - observed
(D) uniformity - scattered
(E) concentration - adaptable

12. Unlike the easily studied neutral and ionized __________ that compose the primary disk of the Milky Way itself, the components of the __________ surrounding our galaxy have proved more resistant to study.

(A) figments - envelope
(B) essences - fluctuations
(C) elements - problems
(D) calculations - perimeter
(E) materials - region

13. Far from being __________, Pat was always __________ to appear acquiescent.

(A) unctuous - loath
(B) brazen - reluctant
(C) ignoble - concerned
(D) obsequious - eager
(E) gregarious - willing

14. Far from undermining the impression of permanent decline, the __________ statue seemed emblematic of its __________ surroundings.

(A) indecorous - opulent
(B) grandiose - ramshackle
(C) pretentious - simple
(D) ungainly - elegant
(E) tawdry - blighted

15. Consumers may choose to purchase fruit, vegetables, meat, and other products from local markets for a range of reasons. They may want to support local producers, rather than the shareholders of large supermarket chains; a local focus that may be regarded as reducing harmful environmental impacts ____________ unnecessary transportation of goods thousands of miles.

(A) to be changed by
(B) from which arises
(C) that are likely to compromise
(D) caused by what could be interpreted as

16. As in other artistic domains, there were those quick to recognize and ____________ sculptures' commercial possibilities. While the magnificent cathedrals of the Middle Ages contained works by the sculptors of the time, it was the combined skills of the stonemason and the architect which were responsible for the structures themselves. In a sense, the reverse has been true in the digital world. The development of hardware and software needed to create and manipulate objects in three-dimensional space has driven by the world of commerces.

(A) extort
(B) extol
(C) exploit
(D) extricate

17. Networks are open structures that develop through the addition of new nodes. They tend to have a more informal nature in comparison with the hierarchical and ordered nature of traditional forms of social relations. Networks are horizontal and reciprocal, more open and flexible, although ultimately they form some more or less stable pattern of social relations. Some of the more postmodern theorists of networks are inclined to make more explicitly anti-realist claims that conflate the existence of networks with epistemological issues, arguing that networks are not epistemological centers and peripheries but a ________________ network of nodes in and through which theorists, theories, and multiple users move and meet.

(A) decentralized
(B) incorporated
(C) functionalized
(D) institutionalized

18. Disgust is a universal human emotion, signaled with its own facial expression and codified everywhere in food taboos. Like all the emotions, disgust has profound effects on human affairs. During World War Ⅱ, American pilots in the Pacific went hungry rather than eat the toads and bugs that they had been taught were perfectly safe. Food aversions are ______________ ethnic markers, persisting long after other traditions have been abandoned.

(A) tenacious
(B) ephemeral
(C) restrained
(D) uncommon

19. From the outset, the concept of freedom of the seas from the proprietary claims of nations was challenged by a contrary notion— that of the __________ of the oceans for reasons of national security and profit.

(A) promotion
(B) exploration
(C) surviving
(D) conservation
(E) enclosure

20. Marshal Philippe Petain, unlike any other French citizen of this century, ahs been paradoxically object of both great veneration and utter __________.

(A) reverence
(B) interest
(C) empathy
(D) contempt
(E) praise

21. One of archaeology's central dilemmas is now to reconstruct the __________ of complex ancient societies from meager and often __________ physical evidence.

(A) riddles - obsolete
(B) details - irrefutable
(C) intricacies - equivocal
(D) patterns - flawless
(E) configuration - explicit

22. In English, the meaning of the word 'tickle' is, so to speak, almost antithetical, employing, as Freud said of the dreamwork, "the same means of representation for expressing contraries." The Oxford English Dictionary cites, among nineteen definitions of the word, the following: "In ___________, easily upset or overthrown, insecure, tottering, crazy .... nicely poised." Other definitions describe a range of experience from excessive credulity to incontinence. The word speaks of the precarious, and so of the erotic. To tickle is, above all, to seduce, often by amusement.

(A) unstable equilibrium
(B) irresistible temptation
(C) inevitable confrontation
(D) unequivocal tranquility

23. The sophistication of the modern world lies not in individual intelligence or imagination. It is a cooperative enterprise. Nobody — literally nobody — knows how to make the pencil on my desk, let alone the computer on which I am writing. The knowledge of how to design, mine, fell, extract, synthesize, combine, manufacture, and market these things is fragmented among thousands, sometimes millions of heads. Once human progress started, it was no longer limited by the size of human brains, Intelligence became ______________.

(A) enlarged and extensive
(B) collective and cumulative
(C) independent and compressed
(D) interdisciplinary and interfacial

24. We have seen that in the span of just over a century, cruel practices that had been a part of civilization for millennia were suddenly abolished. The killing of witches, the torture of prisoners, the persecution of heretics, the execution of nonconformists, and the enslavement of foreigners — all carried out with stomach-turning cruelty — quickly passed from ____________ to ____________. Payne remarks on how difficult it is to explain these changes: "the routes whereby uses of force are abandoned are often quite unexpected, even mysterious. Time and again one encounters violent practices so rooted and so self-reinforcing that it seems almost magical that they were overcome."

(A) blood sports - public hangings
(B) sinful desires - commonplaceness
(C) the unexceptionable - the unthinkable
(D) explicit moral argumentation - unspoken norms

25. In our globalized world, the threats we face are ____________. The rich are vulnerable to the threats that attack the poor, and vice versa. A nuclear terrorist attack on the United States or Europe would have devastating effects on the whole world. But so would the appearance of a new virulent pandemic disease in a poor country with no effective-care system.

(A) immediate
(B) unpredictable
(C) interconnected
(D) underestimated

26. Schlesinger has recently assumed a conciliatory attitude that is not ________ by his colleagues who continue to ________ compromises.

(A) eschewed - dread
(B) shared - defend
(C) questioned - reject
(D) understood - advocate
(E) commended - disparage

27. In the midst of so many evasive comments, this forthright statement, whatever its intrinsic merit, plainly stands out as ________.

(A) a paradigm
(B) a misnomer
(C) a profundity
(D) an inaccuracy
(E) an anomaly

28. Grape fruit juice interacts dangerously with many common medications; only a few sips can turn a ________ dose into one that is ________.

(A) beneficial - reactive
(B) therapeutic - toxic
(C) prescriptive - harmful
(D) detrimental - noxious
(E) curative - salutary

29. Everyone who is lucky enough to live to old age will face the challenge of paying the costs of housing, food, and medical care. The question that our society wrestles with is how we should meet this challenge. In general, conservatives claim that individuals should take responsibility for themselves. From this point of view, people must ensure that they will have the resources they need — through working and a systematic plan to save for their retirement. Liberals claim that ________ is fine for well-off people, but what about those who have not been able to earn enough? From their point of view, a government-centered approach is best. How conservative or liberal you are on this issue may come down to this: to what extent do you think higher-income people should help provide ____________ for lower-income people?

(A) self-sacrifice - sustainable welfare
(B) self-reliance - economic security
(C) self-discipline - emotional stability
(D) self-determination - material independence

30. The skeleton of ________ bird that was recently discovered indicated that this ancient creature _______ today's birds in that, unlike earlier birds and unlike reptilian ancestors, it had a tooth in its head.

(A) a primeval - obscured
(B) a unique - preempted
(C) a primitive - anticipated
(D) a contemporary - foreshadowed
(E) an advanced - differed from

31. Marx explains '①________________,' that is, he describes the imperative of the social structure that facilitates and constrains social action, but he does not explain '②________________,' the mechanics of capital's motion. Foucault explains, '②__________,' that is, he describes the mechanics of power, but he does not explain '①______________,' the motive or purpose of disciplinary power. If Marx's *explicandum* is a cluster of conclusion in search of a premise, then Foucault's explicans is a cluster of premises in search of a conclusion.

(A) ① how - ② what
(B) ① why - ② what
(C) ① why - ② how
(D) ① what - ② how

32. Across all social classes, parents pay close attention to their children's education. Working-class and poor parents are no less eager than middle-class parents to see their children succeed in school. They take a different approach to helping them reach that goal, however. Working-class and poor parents often fear doing "the wrong thing" in school-related matters. They tent to be much more respectful of educators' professional experiences than are their middle-class counterparts. Thus, working-class and poor parents typically are ______________ rather than ______________ toward school personnel; they seek guidance from educators rather than giving advice to them; and they try to maintain a separation between school and home rather than foster an interconnectedness.

(A) indifferent - skeptical
(B) frustrated - gratifying
(C) deferential - demanding
(D) clangorous - encouraging

33. Though he wasn't particularly well-known as a humanitarian, his deep sense of responsibility for those who were suffering was real, and was belied by an outward appearance of ________.

(A) bliss
(B) mirth
(C) smartness
(D) indifference

34. Daniel, not a(n) ________ by nature, refused to ________ his ideals for a quicker and more expedient solution to the problems plaguing his community.

(A) conformist - invoke
(B) organizer - denounce
(C) opportunist - compromise
(D) authoritarian - revamp

35. Pastiche will often be an imitation not of a single text, but of the ________ possibilities of texts.

(A) proportionate
(B) premonitory
(C) indefinite
(D) insolvent
(E) discarding

36. In our computer-dominated world, it can make us nervous to consider our own clumsy capabilities. Is there anything we're good at that computers aren't better at? Are machines making us ________________? Are our hard drives secretly laughing at us up their electronic sleeves? According to researchers, there still are a few skills in which humans ________________ superiority over computers. We're better at pattern recognition. We are capable of emotional connections. We're more innovative.

(A) obsolete - retain
(B) subversive - plummet
(C) rampant - invigorate
(D) dogmatic - acknowledge
(E) nebulous - emphasize

37. Nikolai Gogol was writing stories that maintained subjective experiences and points of view, often mingling reality with a dream-like, fantastical world. Limited points of view — as opposed to ____________, omniscient third-person — allowed the reader to see the world of the story through a(n) ____________ perspective.

(A) multiplied - slanted
(B) singular - egalitarian
(C) objective - skewed
(D) indifferent - impartial
(E) transcendent - sublime

38. Although there are differences among individual tribes, distinct motifs are clearly discernible in the sculptures of the Pacific Northwest tribes. Symbolizing cultural and religious beliefs, tribal sculpture focuses primarily on human and animal figures. But more significantly, the art is highly __________. Sculptors utilize certain culturally recognized features to identify the subject. To portray a beaver, the artist may carve two elongated front teeth and a tail clearly marked with scales. To create a hawk, the artist may sculpt a long curving beak reaching back to touch the hawk's face. These stylized features may then be arranged by the artist according to the aesthetic needs of the sculpture to depict the ideas or impressions the artist wishes to convey.

(A) impressionistic
(B) caricatural
(C) extemporaneous
(D) iconographic

39. Fear is, of course, a normal response to danger, i.e., real danger, and results in a conditioned mode of response — flight, anxiety, or caution, etc. But the little child is most intensively afraid of many imaginary dangers as well as real dangers. There has been a considerable amount of argument among psychologists as to what may constitute ______________ to a young child.

(A) a fear-provoking situation
(B) the non-committal imagination
(C) the conscious levels of the mind
(D) a response to inner stimuli

40. Political Economy or Economics is a study of mankind in the ordinary business of life; it examines that part of individual and social action which is most closely connected with the attainment and with the use of the material requisites of wellbeing. Thus it is on the one side a study of ___________; and on the other, and more important side, a part of the study of ___________. For man's character has been moulded by his every-day work, and the material resources which he thereby procures, more than by any other influence unless it be that of his religious ideals.

(A) wealth - man
(B) welfare - capitalism
(C) society - religion
(D) class - parity

UNIT 2 역 접

역접의 표현

But

Nevertheless

Yet

Even if(though)/Although/Though

In spite of

On the other hand

The other way around

The fact(truth) is ~

the opposite

Instead(Rather)

Unfortunately

Fortunately

Of course

Indeed, In fact, In reality

In effect

However

Nevertheless/Nonetheless/Still/Even so

Despite/for all/with all/notwithstanding

all the same

The problem(difficulty/trouble) is ~

on the contrary

while

conversely

reversedly

surprisingly

Instead/Rather

paradoxically

ironically

예시문제

1. Despite the efforts made by the municipal government to increase public transportation usage, many people of the city continued to drive their own vehicles, complaining that the bus schedules were too __________ to be relied upon.

(A) exacting
(B) circuitous
(C) rigid
(D) isolated
(E) erratic

2. Even though car owners are sometimes extremely __________ of automobile repair shops as a whole, they are unwilling to treat their own mechanics with equal criticism.

(A) reverential
(B) deferential
(C) redemptive
(D) disdainful
(E) trusting

3. Even though the survey was designated as an interdisciplinary course, it involved no real __________ of subject matter.

(A) encapsulation
(B) organization
(C) synthesis
(D) discussion
(E) verification

4. No feasibility study, environmental-impact report, business case or financing plan has yet been released. Instead come ________________ from the Sandinista government of Daniel Ortega about how it will bring a jobs bonanza and end poverty.

(A) qualms
(B) barographs
(C) platitudes
(D) misgivings

5. Marcus Eriksen, of the Five Gyres Institute in Los Angeles, worked with an international team of colleagues to build an oceanographic model of floating debris to estimate the amount of plastic in the sea. The results, published this week in PLOS ONE, found that just over 75% of the 268,940 tons of plastic is accounted for by items measuring more than 200mm. As for the number of items in the sea, the researchers calculated this to be 5.25 trillion bits of plastic of all sizes.

The vast majority, some 4.8 trillion, are microplastics and these were spread across the world. ______________ the number of microplastics appears huge, it was much lower than the researchers expected. The smallest microplastics ought to be more abundant than larger ones, because the tiny ones are continually being degraded into fragments thanks to the effects of sunlight and other weathering processes. ________________, suggesting that some other mechanisms are removing the smallest particles from the oceans' surface.

(A) Even though — Additional research confirmed this idea
(B) Although — In fact the opposite was true
(C) Because — However, research proved the contrary
(D) In fact — But results contradicted this notion

6. ________________, In the past few years a new generation of artist, graphic designers and others accustomed to digital life has rediscovered a process barely changed since its invention by Johannes Gutenberg over 500 years ago. Letterpress is "so old it's new", writes David Jury, whose book on the topic is subtitled "The allure of the handmade". Even MOO, an online maker of business cards, has just unveiled eight letterpress designs.

(A) Printing has undergone radical innovations in recent years
(B) The printing press completely transformed the landscape of modern European history
(C) Traditional hand printing is set to overtake laser printing in the next decade
(D) For all the fetishizing, this turn back towards hand printing is real and widespread

7. In the 1991 Gulf war Iraq's armed forces used American-made color photocopiers to produce their battle plans, ________________. The circuitry in some of them contained concealed transmitters that revealed their position to American electronic-warfare aircraft, making bomb and missile strikes more precise. The operation highlights a secret front in high-tech warfare: turning enemy assets into liabilities.

(A) The machine didn't work well
(B) That was a mistake
(C) The story cannot be true
(D) That's not the way it goes
(E) That was all right anyway

8. High software prices are frequently said to __________ widespread illegal copying, although the opposite-that high prices are the cause of the copying-is equally plausible.

(A) contribute to
(B) result from
(C) correlate with
(D) explain
(E) precede

9. Arruthers' latest literary criticism __________ her reputation for trenchant commentary: despite its intriguing title and the fulsome praise on its dust jacket, it is nothing more than a collection of __________.

(A) reinforces - pronouncements
(B) belies - platitudes
(C) prejudices - insights
(D) advances - aphorisms
(E) undermines - judgments

10. Despite the fact that it is almost universally __________, the practice of indentured servitude still __________ in many parts of the world.

(A) condemned - abates
(B) tolerated - survives
(C) proscribed - persists
(D) mandated - lingers
(E) disdained - intervenes

11. A unique clay disk found at the Minoan site of Phaistos is often ________________ as the earliest example of printing by scholars who have defended its claim to this status despite equivalent claims put forward for other printing artifacts.

(A) questioned
(B) overlooked
(C) adduced
(D) conceded
(E) dismissed

12. Despite its many ___________, the whole-language philosophy of teaching reading continues to gain ______________ among educators.

(A) detractors - notoriety
(B) adherents - prevalence
(C) critics - currency
(D) enthusiasts - popularity
(E) practitioners - credibility

13. Though extremely ____________ about his own plans, the man allowed his associates no such privacy and was constantly ____________ information about what they intended to do next.

(A) idiosyncratic - altering
(B) guarded - eschewing
(C) candid - uncovering
(D) reticent - soliciting
(E) fastidious - ruining

14. However ______________ they might be, Roman poets were bound to have some favorite earlier author whom they would ______________.

(A) subservient - imitate
(B) independent - inspire
(C) original - emulate
(D) creative - admire
(E) talented - neglect

15. Although Irish literature continued to flourish after the sixteenth century, a ______________ tradition is ______________ in the visual arts: we think about Irish culture in terms of the word, not in terms of pictorial images.

(A) rich - superfluous
(B) lively - found
(C) comparable - absent
(D) forgotten - apparent
(E) lost - extant

16. Although the meanings of words may necessarily be liable to change, it does not follow that the lexicographer is therefore unable to render spelling, in a great measure, ______________.

(A) arbitrary
(B) superfluous
(C) interesting
(D) flexible
(E) constant

17. Modern animal psychiatrists argue that there is no evidence of an animal knowingly attempting suicide in the wild. Researchers now know that the mass deaths of lemmings are an unfortunate consequence of a dense population of creatures emigrating together at the same time. In cases where a pet dies following its master's death, this can be explained by the disruption of a social tie. The animal does not __________ to die; instead, the animal was so used to its master that it no longer accepts food from anther individual. "To think it died from suicide like a person after the death of a spouse is just a projection of a style of romantic human interpretation."

(A) follow a bad arrangement
(B) make a conscious decision
(C) have a clear preference
(D) agree easily
(E) reveal a hidden desire

18. Companies devote a lot of thought to sending people abroad. They offer foreign postings to their most promising employees. They sweeten the deal with higher salaries and big allowances, and sometimes help to find work for spouses. But when it comes to ______________, it is a different story. One study suggests that a quarter of firms provide no help for repatriates at all. Many others offer at best a few links to websites.

(A) paying a bonus
(B) being promoted in the company
(C) extending the stay in a foreign country
(D) sending the employees abroad
(E) bringing the employees home

19. Although it seems __________ that there would be a greater risk of serious automobile accidents in densely populated areas, such accidents are more likely to occur in sparsely populated regions.

(A) paradoxical
(B) axiomatic
(C) anomalous
(D) irrelevant
(E) portentous

20. Although a few delegates gave the opposition's suggestions a __________ response, most greeted the statement of a counterposition with __________.

(A) favorable - approval
(B) dispirited - reluctance
(C) surly - resentment
(D) halfhearted - composure
(E) vitriolic - civility

21. Although normally __________, Alison felt so strongly about the issue that she put aside her reserve and spoke up at the committee meeting.

(A) diffident
(B) contentious
(C) facetious
(D) presumptuous
(E) intrepid

22. The accusations we bring against others should be ___________ ourselves; they should not __________ complacency and easy judgments on our part concerning our own moral conduct.

(A) definitions of - produce
(B) instructions to - equate
(C) denigrations of - exclude
(D) warning to - justify
(E) parodies of - satirize

23. The trick for Michael was to ___________ his son an illusory orderliness; only alone at night, when the boy was asleep, could Michael ___________ the chaos he kept hidden from his son.

(A) explore with - demonstrate
(B) conjure for - acknowledge
(C) conceal from - dispel
(D) demystify for - escape
(E) endure with - abandon

24. He had expected gratitude for his disclosure, but instead he encountered __________ bordering on hostility.

(A) patience
(B) discretion
(C) openness
(D) ineptitude
(E) indifference

25. Bird flu has killed more than 330 people since 2003. That may not sound many, but it amounts to 60% of the 570 known cases of the disease. The only reason the death toll is not higher is that those who succumbed caught the virus directly from a bird. Fortunately for everyone else, it does not pass easily from person to person. ___________. That is the burden of research carried out last year by two teams of scientists. They tweaked the bird-flu virus's genes to produce a version which can travel through the air from ferret to ferret. And ferrets are good proxies for people.

(A) Of course not
(B) But it might
(C) That's it
(D) It doesn't matter
(E) Or nothing else

26. ______________________, splendid in itself, cannot be fully reconciled with the need for planning, organization, careful and responsible calculation. The pursuit of truth — the noblest of aims — cannot be fully reconciled with the happiness that men desire, for even if I know that I have some incurable disease of pursuing truth, this will not make me happier or freer. I must always choose: between peace and excitement, or knowledge and blissful ignorance.

(A) Mercy
(B) Justice
(C) Spontaneity
(D) Voluntary action

27. The necessity of establishing discrete categories for observations frequently leads to attempts to make absolute ____________ when there are in reality only ____________.

(A) analyses - hypotheses
(B) correlations - digressions
(C) distinctions - gradations
(D) complications - ambiguities
(E) conjectures - approximations

28. Although he was undoubtedly obligated to corporate interests due to his sponsors' sizable contributions to his campaign, the candidate presented a platform that ____________ his allegiance to those companies' agendas.

(A) belied
(B) averred
(C) entrenched
(D) corroborated

29. The renowned painter often behaved unpleasantly, but his actions were ____________ by others because of his ____________ abilities.

(A) condoned - virtuosic
(B) minimized - dubious
(C) overlooked - mundane
(D) abused - musical
(E) chastised - impressive

30. I was four, playing outside in the humid Kentucky air. I saw my grandfather's truck and thought, "Granddad shouldn't have to drive such an ugly truck." Then I spied a gallon of paint. Idea! I got a brush and painted white polka dots all over the truck. I was on the roof finishing the job when he walked up, looking as if he were in a trance. "Angela, that's the prettiest truck I've ever seen!" Sometimes I think adults don't stop to see things through a child's eyes. He could have crushed me. ______________.

(A) Instead, he lifted my little soul
(B) My dreams, however, came true
(C) He thus turned a deaf ear to my wishes
(D) In the end, I blossomed into a renowned artist

31. The principal engine of economic development is the work and creativity of individuals. What induces them to strive and invent is a climate of liberty that leaves them in control of their own destiny. If individuals feel that others are responsible for them, the effort of individuals will __________. If others tell them what to think and believe, the consequence is either a loss of motivation and creativity or a choice between submission or rebellion. However, neither submission nor rebellion generates development. Submission leaves a society without ____________ and rebellion diverts energies away from constructive effort toward resistance.

(A) ebb- innovators
(B) diminish - dictators
(C) be truncated - poverty
(D) be maximized - preeminence

32. Dorothy Parker's biting wit earned her great fame, but she was eventually fired from Vanity Fair because the magazine's editors disapproved of her excessively __________ style.

(A) timorous
(B) convoluted
(C) hackneyed
(D) florid
(E) caustic

33. Georgia O'Keefe's ability to paint was ____________ by vision problems toward the end of her career, but she ____________, working in pencil and charcoal until she was more than ninety years old.

(A) rectified - procrastinated
(B) marred - deviated
(C) complemented - persisted
(D) averted - commemorated
(E) compromised - persevered

34. The Olympic Games were banned in A.D. 393 by Theodosius I, but Europeans continued to hold them in spite of that ________________.

(A) prohibition
(B) delay
(C) embellishment
(D) rebellion
(E) threat

35. While Kepler was the first person to ____________ a system that correctly described planetary motion, he did not succeed in ________________ a complete theory.

(A) invent – refuting
(B) imagine – overturning
(C) disprove – validating
(D) devise – formulating
(E) develop – revoking

36. Reading has historically been an exclusive exchange between the reader and the words on the page, but interactive technologies have transformed it into a far less ____________ activity.

(A) comprehensive
(B) isolated
(C) intense
(D) collaborative
(E) nostalgic

37. Even if the ____________ in the authoritarian regime are sincere in their desire for democratic reform, they are unlikely to bring about immediate change.

(A) ambassadors
(B) dissidents
(C) loyalists
(D) denizens
(E) mercenaries

38. While many outside the company have attributed the company's success to the president's prescience, insiders realized that this success owed more to the president's inflexibility than to any ____________ that the president might have displayed.

(A) foresight
(B) obduracy
(C) popularity
(D) perseverance

39. Despite significant advances in research about women, the role of female labor remains the single most glaring omission in most economic analyses of the history of European industrialization. Women far outnumbered men as workers in textile industries, yet wage indices and discussions of growth, cost of living and the like ________________ about the male labor force.

(A) replicate facts
(B) too rarely talk
(C) incorporate data only
(D) suppress most information

40. Although bound to uphold the law, a judge is free to use discretion to ____________ to cruel severity of some criminal penalties.

(A) enforce
(B) reinstate
(C) mitigate
(D) provoke

41. Even today there are more than 2,500 train stations in Britain, generating more than 6 million possible journeys. It is not possible to computerize that many journeys, nor would it be ①__________ to do so. Many those possible journeys are never undertaken; given that only ten people boarded a train at Buckenham in Norfolk in 2007, and only fifteen got off at Coombe Junction Halt, in Cornwall, it is most ②__________ that anyone travelled from Buckenham to Coombe Junction Halt. The speed of trains between these two places is ③__________ to an understanding of how the railways performed, although faster trains might lead to this journey becoming more common.

(A) ① reasonable – ② improbable – ③ convincing
(B) ① sensible – ② unlikely – ③ irrelevant
(C) ① impractical – ② improbable – ③ unmistakable
(D) ① unthinkable – ② certain – ③ misleading

42. The trend toward what some historians have called the 'Imperial Presidency' started early in the twentieth century with the activist presidency of Theodore Roosevelt, and reached its ______________ under President Franklin D. Roosevelt, who planned and implemented his New Deal policies despite considerable opposition from Congress and the Supreme Court.

(A) goal
(B) apogee
(C) epitome
(D) consensus

43. Use of ecological theory for management of nature needs to follow different rules than use of physical theory to build shyscrapers or rockets. Whereas an engineer has a firm concept of stresses in constructing a structure of steel girders or thrust required to carry a rocket payload, an ecologist has nothing comparable. In such cases, the theory can guide insight, but the insight must be ____________ by local understanding of how well the organisms in question fit the assumptions of the relevant model. A manager must also realize that even if a population could in theory be managed for sustainable yield or maintained in habitat fragments of different sizes, populations might usually be so small that firm estimates and therefore predictions of persistence, extinction, or colonization are ____________.

If a Himalayan valley hosts three snow leopards, a manager of the cats and their prey may benefit from understanding that the local population may disappear and be replaced by other individuals or that the cats may simply trade individuals with other valleys. The capacity to actually estimate turnover on a quantitative basis is quite likely out of reach.

(A) tempered - infeasible
(B) consolidated - improbable
(C) strengthened - presumable
(D) moderated - conceivable

44. Although there exists no totalizing principle to unify the diverse perspectives shaping market interpretation, there are a few ____________ principles that are agile enough to be deployed within a wide field of analytical approaches.

(A) quizzical
(B) quiescent
(C) mercurial
(D) heuristic

45. A legend can endure forever in the collective imagination, and can have amazing ______________ in spite of repeated attempts to disprove it. The tale of Atlantis is such a survivor. Thousands of books have been written speculating where Atlantis was located. All of this is in spite of a legion of failed efforts to find evidence that the land ever existed. The failure to find Atlantis is not for a lack of effort on anyone's part. Archeologists, geophysicists, and seafaring explorers have all tried to find some trace of the lost city. One author who has written extensively on the subject has said that the reason the belief in Atlantis still persists is that it is difficult to prove ______________. One can't produce evidence that something never existed.

(A) longevity – a negative
(B) popularity – an axiom
(C) expansion – a principle
(D) authority – a syllogism

46. Although the film critic was ______________ in her conviction that sequels are generally inferior to their predecessors, she did acknowledge occasional exceptions such as The Godfather Part Ⅱ, a film she considered superior to the original.

(A) avionic
(B) svelte
(C) disconsolate
(D) adamant

47. We need to have our young people follow rules and regulations, but the application of those rules and regulations needs to be ________________ by common sense.

(A) titillated
(B) tempered
(C) amassed
(D) abrogated

48. Many critics of Emily Bronte's novel *Wuthering Heights* see its second part as a counterpoint that comments on, if it does not reverse, the first part, where a romantic reading receives more confirmation. Seeing the two parts as a whole is encouraged by the novel's sophisticated structure, revealed in its complex use of narrators and time shifts. Granted that the presence of these elements need not argue for an authorial awareness of novelistic construction comparable to Henry James, their presence does encourage attempts to unify the novel's ______________ parts. However, any interpretation that seeks to unify all of the novel's diverse elements is bound to be somewhat unconvincing. This is because *Wuthering Heights* has recalcitrant elements of undeniable power that, ultimately, resist ________________ in an all-encompassing interpretation.

(A) multifarious – privation
(B) parallel – debarment
(C) heterogenous – inclusion
(D) punctilious – duress

49. The ___________ villagers touched their caps in front of her but sneered behind her back.

(A) obsequious
(B) winsome
(C) intrepid
(D) effulgent

50. The ___________ garter snake, often spotted in yards, parks, and gardens, is sometimes mistaken for a venomous snake.

(A) inveterate
(B) ingenuous
(C) innocuous
(D) inane

UNIT 3 시간을 이용한 대조

시간을 이용한 대조의 표현

Today, Now	in the past
recently	nowadays, these days
As a child	used to
previously	no longer
formerly	at one time
heretofore(hitherto)	in days gone by
precedently(antecedently)	once
initial(initially)	until now
	at first
	after
	before

예 시 문 제

1. After naturally occurring smallpox was eradicated, the World Health Organization chose to ________________ the remaining samples of the virus in hopes that they might be later used in developing means to combat other viruses.

(A) eliminate
(B) duplicate
(C) retain
(D) extirpate
(E) cultivate

2. The popularity of pseudoscience and quack medicines in the nineteenth century suggests that people were very ____________, but the gullibility of the public today makes citizens of yesterday look like hard-nosed ______________.

(A) cautions - educators
(B) sophisticated - realists
(C) rational - pragmatists
(D) naive - idealists
(E) credulous - skeptics

3. The media once portrayed the governor as anything but ineffective; they now, however, make her out to be the epitome of ______________.

(A) altruism
(B) brilliance
(C) dynamism
(D) fecklessness

4. The migrant question is a more serious threat to Europe's future than anything in recent memory, because it can't be resolved by a promise from a central bank or an infusion of someone else's cash. This is a question of Europe's identity — and whether it means as much to European voters as it did a generation ago. ________________, the refugees will keep coming, and it will become harder for governments to make sacrifices to welcome them.

(A) All the while
(B) On the one hand
(C) In conclusion
(D) On the other hand
(E) By the way

5. Half a century ago doctors saw the fetus as a 'perfect parasite' — absorbing what it needed but sealed off in the womb from any harm done to the mother. About half of American women smoked through pregnancy. When babies were born with the damage now described as fetal-alcohol syndrome, ________________ was blamed. Since then it has become a commonplace that healthy habits and good nutrition during pregnancy make it less likely that a baby will be born early, underweight or ill. Now a growing body of research is showing that problems caused by the prenatal environment may not be apparent at birth, but can resonate throughout life.

(A) smoking
(B) drinking
(C) stress
(D) heredity
(E) infection

6. Martin Luther King, Jr. was one of the greatest speechmakers, and at first it might seem obvious why. As well as being educated and prodigiously talented, the young reverend left nothing to ________________. Every syllable of his oratory was meticulously prepared. By contrast, consider the fate of those who do not seem to have prepared. Rick Perry, then the governor of Texas, was once the favorite to be the Republican presidential nominee for the 2012 election. His chances ebbed because his performance in debates was ____________. During one debate, a journalist tweeted, "I think Rick Perry just had a stroke."

(A) risk – raging
(B) chance – excruciating
(C) speculation – disappointing
(D) coincidence – impassioned

7. The fortress-like facade of the Museum of Cartoon Art seems calculated to remind visitors that the comic strip is an art form that has often been ___________ by critics.

(A) charmed
(B) assailed
(C) unnoticed
(D) exhilarated
(E) overwhelmed

8. Our biological uniqueness requires that the effects of substance must be verified by ________________ experiments, even after thousands of tests of the effects of that substance on animals.

(A) controlled
(B) random
(C) replicated
(D) human
(E) evolutionary

9. In the past, popular religious groups functioned ______________. This is no longer the case. Paralleling, and in some ways reinforcing, the impact of post-modernism, is that of globalization. In the context of the spread of ideas, expecially religious views, globalization — particularly the impact of the spread of communication to all parts of the world — means that groups are no longer isolated. The global and widespread change causes religion to be increasingly pushed out of the public arena into the private domain. In the past, when ________________ in religious traditions came, the breakaways were either recaptured or, if they stayed independent, came in time to reflect again the diversity from which they wished to escape. Today, in contrast, such divisions are less easily contained, as the erosion of Catholicism in Latin America, for instance, where it is giving way to Protestant Charismatic religions, seems to indicate.

(A) in isolation - breaks
(B) in the secular West - a focal point
(C) in the private domain - solidarities
(D) in multifaceted communication - unshakable convictions

10. Early studies often concluded that the public was ___________ the propagandistic influence of mass communications, but one recent study indicates that, on the contrary, mass communications seldom produce marked changes in social attitudes or actions.

(A) unaware of
(B) coping with
(C) susceptible to
(D) unimpressed by

11. Giant pandas used to live in large areas of China, but they are now close to ______________. In the past, they were spread throughout the forests of southern and eastern China. Each panda needed a large area of forest — and large amounts of bamboo — but there was enough forest and bamboo for tens of thousands of giant pandas. However, in the twentieth century, people moved into the forests and cut down the bamboo. By the 1990s, scientists estimated that there were only about 1,000 wild pandas left. Fortunately, the Chinese government decided to try to save them. It created several panda ______________, where the pandas and their forests were protected.

(A) exile - infringements
(B) undertaking - edifices
(C) collapse - inklings
(D) evaporation - manipulations
(E) extinction - reserves

12. We were amazed that a man who had been heretofore the most ____________ of public speakers could, in a single speech, electrify an audience and bring them cheering to their feet.

(A) pedestrian
(B) enthralling
(C) auspicious
(D) versatile

13. Beginning in the 1780s, Charlotte Smith's explicit and implicit criticism of English life and laws earned her a reputation as a "____________________." Her novels contain some of the earliest literary attacks on the English legal system. In comparison to later exposes by ninteenth-century novelists such as Charles Dickens, Charlotte Smith's attacks appear somewhat timorous. However, it cannot be denied that it was Smith who introduced such a target for later novelists and that when she did, her action was considered so audacious that it laid her open to the charge ofbeing a "____________________."

(A) mediator - tyrant
(B) reformer - conformer
(C) subversive - menace
(D) cleric - forerunner

14. Nearly ____________ by disease and the destruction of their habitat, koalas are now found only in isolated parts of eucalyptus forest.

(A) sublimed
(B) decimated
(C) infuriated
(D) averted

정답과 해설

Part Ⅰ	같은 방향
Part Ⅱ	다른 방향

Part Ⅰ 같은 방향

UNIT 1 인과관계

예 시 문 제

1. 정답 : (A)

해석 : 그녀는 매우 **말이 없었기** 때문에, Mary는 사람들 속에서 거의 말을 하지 않았다.

이종현T의 Logical Point

부사절의 she와 주절의 Mary는 같은 대상이다. 따라서 주절에서 Mary가 거의 말을 하지 않았다 라고 했으므로 부사절엔 그녀는 말을 하지 않는 것과 관련이 있는 내용이 들어가야 한다. 따라서 정답은 (A) reticent 이다.

2. 정답 : (C)

해석 : 마을 사람들은 노상강도를 너무 철저하게 **궤멸시켜서**, 그 생존자들의 대부분은 눈물 없이는 무기를 다시는 못 들었다.

이종현T의 Logical Point

노상강도를 '빈칸' 했더니 그 결과 강도들 중 생존자들이 무기를 다시 들기 힘들 정도가 되었다는 것이므로 강도들은 마을 사람들에게 졌다는 의미의 내용이 필요하다. 따라서 정답은 (C) routed가 된다.

3. 정답 : (A)

해석 : 대부분의 사람들이 Davis의 책을 충격적이라고 생각하는 것은 우연이 아니다, 왜냐하면 이것은 그들이 오랫동안 **소중하게 여겨왔던** 수많은 믿음들을 약화시키도록 **계산되어졌기** 때문이다.

이종현T의 Logical Point

첫 문장에 Davis의 책은 충격적이라고 나와 있다. 그리고 두번째 문장에는 믿음을 약화시켰다는 것이므로 그들이 믿었던 것들을 약화시키도록 만들기 때문에 충격적이 되는 것이다. 고로 정답은 (A)가 된다.

4. 정답 : (D)

해석 : 충분히 적절하게도, 시간과 스타일을 변화시키는 것에 대한 개념으로 가득 찬 이 작품은 수년 동안 지속적으로 **개정되어져왔다**, 그렇게 함으로써 이것의 변덕을 반영했다.

이종현T의 Logical Point

분사구문은 앞 문장과 같은 내용이 되어야 하는데 분사구문 내용이 변덕을 반영했다고 나와 있다. 따라서 앞 문장도 변화한다는 내용이 필요하고 정답은 (D) revised가 된다.

5. 정답 : (B)

해석 : 초기 미국 작가들은 위대한 문학의 표시는 보통의 연설에서는 발견되지 않는 웅장함과 우아함이라고 생각했기 때문에, 그들은 일반적인 말을 **피했다**.

이종현T의 Logical Point

보통의 연설에서는 할 수 없는 우아하고 웅장한 말들에 대해 말하고 있으므로, 주절에 나와 있는 보통의 말인 vernacular은 좋아하지 않는 것이다. 따라서 정답은 (B) avoided가 된다.

6. 정답 : (B)

해석 : 역설적으로, 비유적인 언어의 적절한 사용은 가장 기본적인 의미에 기초해야만 한다, 왜냐하면 이러한 **글자 그대로의** 의미를 인식하지 못하는 것이 혼합된 비유와 그것들에 수반되는 부조화를 야기시키기 때문이다.

이종현T의 Logical Point

첫문장의 denotative meaning과 같은 의미의 말이 빈칸에 와야 한다. 왜냐하면 필자가 말하는 인식해야 하는 것은 denotative meaning이기 때문이다. 따라서 정답은 (B) literal이 된다.

7. 정답 : (D)

해석 : 오늘날 물은 조경술에서는 그 어느때보다도 **여기저기 존재한다**, 왜냐하면 기술적인 진보들은 인공 폭포를 공공장소에 설치하는 것을 몇몇 경우에는 심지어 **의무적이게**, 그리고 쉽게 했기 때문이다.

이종현T의 Logical Point

일단 첫번째 빈칸을 추론하기 위해 because 뒤를 보면 인공 폭포를 설치하는 것을 쉽게 했으므로 물은 더 자주 보인다는 의미의 ubiquitous가 들어가야 한다. 그리고 두번째 빈칸은 인공 폭포를 설치하는 것을 쉽게 만드는 것을 넘어서서 더 어떻게 한다는 의미이므로 obligatory가 들어가서 설치는 하고 싶을 때 쉽게 할 수 있게 하는 것을 넘어서서 무조건 설치하게 했다는 의미를 만들어줘야 한다. 고로 정답은 (D)가 된다.

8. 정답 : (A)

➡ 해석 : 치열한 경쟁사회에서 버텨내기 위해 노력하면서 사람들은 엄청나게 긴 시간동안 뼈 빠지게 일하고 있다. 미국에서 상류층이 되지 못하는 결과는 너무나 커서, 그 결과 치열한 경쟁은 **더 심해진다**. 승자가 모든 것을 가져가는 사회에서는 이러한 시간부족 현상을 예상할 수 있다.

➡ 이종현T의 Logical Point

첫번째 문장에서 경쟁사회에서 사람들은 더 열심히 일한다는 내용이 나왔고 이어지는 문장도 계속 같은 내용이 나와야 한다. 그렇다면 두번째 문장에서 상류층이 되지 못하는 결과는 너무 크다는 것은 매우 좋지 않다는 것이고 그래서 경쟁은 더 악화되고 심해진다는 내용이 오는 것이 맞다. 따라서 정답은 (A) exacerbated가 된다.

9. 정답 : (D)

➡ 해석 : 그들의 이야기의 높은 진중함은 부분적으로 그들의 형이상학으로부터 발생되었기 때문에, 남쪽 지역 작가들은 그들의 **철학적인** 소질로 인정받았다.

➡ 이종현T의 Logical Point

metaphysics가 무엇인지 아는게 중요한 문제였다. 형이상학이라는 것은 세계의 궁극적 근거를 연구한다는 점에서 철학과 관련이 깊은 것이기에 정답은 (D)가 된다.

10. 정답 : (B)

➡ 해석 : 강박적 소비 현상, 지루함에 대한 두려움, 도피에 대한 갈망 등이 '키치(kitsch)'라 불리는 것의 증가에 다양한 정도와 형태로 **기여해온** 요인들에 속한다. 키치는 근대성의 가장 전형적인 산물들 가운데 하나이다. 그러나 이것만으로는 근대성, 아방가르드, 데카당스의 사상들과 **나란히 함께** 키치를 논해야할 이유로 충분하지 않을 것이다. 이들 사상은 한편으로 시간이라는 **공통된** 주제를 통해 긴밀히 연관되어 있지만, 또 다른 한편으로는 그 범위가(키치보다) 훨씬 더 넓기 때문이다.

➡ 이종현T의 Logical Point

첫번째 빈칸은 주어가 결과인지, 주어가 원인인지를 보는 것이 중요하다. 그런데 다음 문장에서 Kitsch가 결과물이라고 나와 있으므로 첫번째 문장에서도 주어가 원인이 된다. 따라서 contribute to가 적절하다. 그리고 두, 세번째 빈칸은 Kitsch와 다른 modernity를 같이 볼 것이냐 말 것이냐의 문제에 관한 이야기이기 때문에 두번째 빈칸에는 along with 그리고 세 번째 빈칸에는 common이 와서 정답은 (B)가 된다.

11. 정답 : (A)

해석 : 하버드 교수인 David Keith는 큰 화산 분출에 의해 던져진 유황층에 의해 만들어졌던 층과 유사한 성층권에 안계의 인공 층으로부터 태양 빛을 반사하는 방법을 연구해왔다. 그리고 이러한 것은 지구를 시원하게 만드는 것으로 알려졌다. 위험들 중 하나는 그러한 분자들이 오존층을 **감소시키는** 화학적 반응을 장려할 수 있다는 것이다. Dr. Keith와 그의 동료들은 그러한 반응의 속도가 어떻게 분자의 크기와 수증기의 수준에 달려있는지를 연구하기를 원했다. 그것들은 위험성을 조사하고 그것들을 제한할 수 있는 발견들을 아마 찾게 도와줄 것이다. 그들은 하늘에 20킬로 위헤 있는 큰 풍선 아래에 걸려있다. 이것은 유황 분자의 **기둥**을 만들 것이고 물리적이고 화학적인 변화를 측정할 것이다.

이종현T의 Logical Point

이 문제를 풀이하는 핵심은 첫번째 빈칸이다. 첫번째 빈칸은 화학적인 반응이 오존층에 주는 영향에 대한 빈칸이고 그 뒤를 보면 그런 화학적인 반응을 제한한다는 내용이 나와 있다. 따라서 오존층에는 안 좋은 영향을 준다는 것을 알 수 있고 정답은 deplete, decrease, diminish가 가능하다. 이 중에 두번째 빈칸에 들어갔을 때 정확히 되는 것은 기둥이라는 의미이므로 정답은 (A)가 된다.

12. 정답 : (C)

해석 : 그러한 섬세한 협상을 수행하는 기술과 입증된 그녀의 인내심 때문에 선택된 그 외교관은 협상하는 동안에 결정하는 것을 **거부했다**. 왜냐하면 그 시기의 어떤 갑작스러운 결정도 **때가 안 좋을** 수 있었기 때문이다.

이종현T의 Logical Point

지문에서 답의 근거를 찾는 것이 중요하다. 첫번째 빈칸에서 make a decision과 무엇이 어울릴 지를 고민하는 것이 아니라 지문 안에서 단서를 잡아야 한다. 지문에서 외교관은 인내심이 있는 외교관이라고 나온다. 따라서 결정을 할 때에도 신중하게 결정한다는 것을 추론할 수 있다. 따라서 결정을 미루거나 하지 않는다는 의미의 declined같은 단어가 적절하다. 그리고 그 뒤엔 결정을 하지 않는 이유에 대한 내용이 나오면 되는데 가장 적절할 것은 inopportune(시기가 안 좋은)이 된다. 따라서 정답은 (C)가 된다.

13. 정답 : (D)

해석 : 꽤 최근까지 당뇨병에 대한 연구는 일종의 행동을 고수하는 것으로서 그 질병의 **치료법**을 개선시키는 것을 시도해왔다. 주로 왜냐하면 어떤 예방하는 전략들도 전혀 **실현가능할** 가능성이 없을 것 같았기 때문이다.

이종현T의 Logical Point

두번째 빈칸과 첫번째 빈칸에서 단서의 기준을 잡고 가야 한다. 두번째 빈칸의 문장이 좋은 의미라면 예방하는 전략은 무조건 가능하고 좋다는 얘기이므로 첫번째 빈칸에는 예방하는 전략이 들어가야 한다. 반면 안 좋은 의미라면 어떤 예방 전략도 가능하지 않으므로 예방 전략이 아닌 다른 비교되는 대상을 넣어줘야 한다. 근데 첫번째 논리로 접근했을 땐 해당 선지가 없으므로 두번째 논리로 접근하여서 어떤 예방 전략도 실행가능하지 않기 때문에 실제 걸렸을 때 치료법을 개선시키는 것을 시도해왔다고 하는 정답은 (D)가 된다.

14. 정답 : (D)

해석 : 인간의 본질과 긴 거리는 속도 제한을 초과하는 것을 그 주에 있는 **소중한** 전통으로 만들어왔다. 그래서 입법자들은 대중들의 관행에 응하면서 그들이 스피드에 대한 증가된 벌금을 **거절했다**는 것은 놀랄 일이 아니었다.

이종현T의 Logical Point

착각하기가 쉽지만 여기서 핵심은 일단 속도 제한을 위반하는 것이 전통이 되었다는 것이도 acceding to ~ 이부분에서 대중들의 관행에 응한다고 되어 있다. 따라서 거기에 따른다는 것이고 벌금은 증가시키지 않는다는 내용이 필요하다. 그리고 관행에 응하므로 좋은 전통이 된다. 따라서 정답은 (D)가 된다.

15. 정답 : (A)

해석 : 국가 기록 보관소는 너무나도 **분열되어서** 그들이 그들의 연구를 차마 끝까지 할 수 없기 때문에 연구자들에게 알려져서 결코 출판되지 않는 정보들을 포함한다.

이종현T의 Logical Point

그 정보는 차마 끝맺음을 할 수 없는 정보가 된다. 그래서 세상에 공표할 수 없는 정보가 된다. 이런 정보를 받아줄 수 있는 것은 (A) divisive가 된다.

16. 정답 : (C)

해석 : 너무나도 많은 미국에서의 현대소설의 많은 부분은 자서전같다. 그리고 너무나도 많은 자서전들은 허구화되었다. 그래서 그 **장르**들은 대게 **서로 교체할 수 있는** 것 같다.

이종현T의 Logical Point

빈칸 앞 문장들을 보면 소설은 자서전처럼 되었고 자서전은 소설처럼 되었다. 따라서 그 둘이 섞인다는 의미가 결과에 들어가면 된다. 그랬을 때 그 둘을 종합할 수 있는 genres가 첫번째 빈칸에 들어가면 되고 서로 섞인다는 의미의 interchangeable이 들어가서 정답은 (C)가 된다.

17. 정답 : (C)

해석 : 많은 정신요법 의사들의 개척적인 연구의 결과를 **이용하는** 것에 대한 실패는 부분적으로 그러한 발견들의 특별한 본질 때문일 수 있다. 심지어 **중요한** 발견들조차도 유용하지 않을지도 모른다.

이종현T의 Logical Point

두번째 빈칸에 even이 앞에 있으므로 보어와 주어는 반대 관계이다. 따라서 not useful의 반대되는 말인 유용한 같은 말이 들어가면 된다. 그리고 연구의 결과가 유용하고 말고에 관한 이야기이므로 연구 결과를 이용한다고 볼 수 있다. 따라서 첫번째 빈칸에는 이용한다는 이야기가 들어간다. 고로 정답은 (C)가 된다.

18. 정답 : (A)

해석 : 이 책은 학자 또는 철학자들만을 염두에 두고 쓴 책이 아니다. 인간 문화의 가장 근본적인 문제들은 일반적인 인간의 관심사항이다. 그리고 이 문제들을 일반 대중들은 쉽게 이해할 수 있어야 한다. **그러므로**, 나는 모든 전문적인 표현을 피하고, 가능한 한 명확하고 단순하게 나의 생각을 표현하고자 노력했다. 그러나 내가 이 책에서 할 수 있는 것이 내 이론을 증명하는 것보다는 설명하고 예증하는 것이라는 것을 나를 비판하는 사람들은 알아야 한다.

이종현T의 Logical Point

빈칸 앞을 보면 대중들이 쉽게 이해할 수 있어야 하고 뒤에서는 어려운 표현을 피한다고 했으니 인과 관계로 보는 것이 좋다. 따라서 정답은 (A)가 된다.

19. 정답 : (D)

해석 : GM이 사과를 하긴 했지만, 회사의 과실에 대한 인식을 다루거나 이러한 일이 다시 일어나지 않도록 해결책을 제시하는 데는 거의 한 일이 없다고 미국 서던 캘리포니아 대학(USC) 경영학과 아이라 칼브(Ira Kalb) 교수가 말했다. 칼브 교수는 토요타(Toyota)가 '급발진'으로 인해 수백만 대의 자동차를 리콜한 이후 자동차 판매에서 90억 달러의 손해를 보았다고 추정한다. 그 후로 토요타는 충분히 회복되어 지난 2년간 전 세계에서 가장 많은 자동차를 판매한 회사가 되었다. 미국인들은 대개 6년마다 자동차를 구입하므로, GM은 소비자의 **기억상실**로 이득을 볼 수 있을 것이다.

이종현T의 Logical Point

위기가 와도 소비자들은 다시 또 그 제품을 사게 된다는 것이므로 정답은 (D)가 된다.

20. 정답 : (A)

해석 : 오직 자신만이 입증할 수 있는 자신의 의도에 관해서조차도 뛰어난 거짓말쟁이가 되는 것은 어렵다. 의도란 감정에서 나오는 것이고 감정은 얼굴과 몸에 진화된 모습으로 나타난다. 스타니슬라브시키(Stanislavsky) 방법(연기론)의 대가가 아니라면, 감정을 거짓으로 꾸며내는 데 어려움을 겪을 것이다. 사실, 감정은 아마도 꾸며내기가 어렵기 ' 때문에' 진화되었을 것이다. 더군다나, 거짓말은 스트레스가 많고 걱정은 숨길 수 없는 표시를 가지고 있다. —것들이 소위 거짓말 탐지기가 있어야 할 근거가 된다. 그리고 인가들 또한 거짓말 탐지기가 되는 쪽으로 진화했다. 따라서 몇몇 진술이 논리적으로 다른 진술들을 함의(含意)한다는 성가신 사실이 존재한다. 말하는 것들 중 일부는 사실일 것이기 때문에, 항상 자신의 거짓말을 드러낼 위험에 처한다. 유대인 속담에 따르면 거짓말쟁이는 상당한 **기억력**을 소유해야 한다.

이종현T의 Logical Point

했던 말들에서 논리적으로 다른 진술이 나온다고 했으므로 했던 말들에서 틀리는 게 나온다는 것이다. 그렇다면 거짓말을 잘하기 위해선 했던 말을 기억했다고 나와야 하므로 정답은 (A)가 된다.

21. 정답 : (D)

해석 : 극장이 부족하다는 이유 때문에, 그 도시는 아이러니하게 **예상 밖의** 영화도시라고 여겨지게 되었다. 그리고 그 평판은 사업가들이 그곳에 새로운 극장을 짓는 것이 **적절하다고** 믿도록 이끌었다.

이종현T의 Logical Point

ironically가 핵심이다. 즉 극장이 부족하다면 영화 산업이 잘 발달하지 않은 도시가 되는게 일반적인 결론인데 ironically가 있으므로, 극장이 부족하긴 하지만 영화가 잘 발달한 도시라고 보는 것이 좋다. 따라서 첫번째 빈칸에는 예상 밖의 같은 의미가 되는 unlikely가 들어가면 되고, 두번째 빈칸에는 영화도시이므로 사업가들은 그곳에 영화를 짓는다는 개념이 들어가면 된다. 따라서 정답은 (D)가 된다.

22. 정답 : (C)

해석 : 신경성 통증에 대한 양질의 치료법이 의료계에서 지속적으로 시행되지 않는 이유는 치료법을 위한 과학적 연구 결과들을 현재로서는 신뢰할 수 없기 때문인데, 연구들은 연구되는 여러 인구집단에서, 특히 아이들 집단에서, 강한 가변성(다양성)을 포함하고 있어서 그 결과들을 서로 **비교할 수 없게** 만들고 있다.

이종현T의 Logical Point

연구들의 결과가 다양하게 바뀔 수 있다는 내용이 앞에 나와 있으므로 결과들은 비교할 수 없다는 (C)가 정답이 된다.

23. 정답 : (B)

▶ 해석 : 한 문화와 다른 문화를 구별 짓는 가장 중요한 변수는 옷, 주택, 음식 또는 식사예절과 같이 쉽게 눈에 띄는 현상이 아니라 오히려 한 문화가 자신과 다른 문화를 바라보는 방식을 형성하는 근본적인 가치관, 태도, 신념 그리고 세계관이다. 의식의 차원 아래에 있는 이러한 요인들이 문화의 상당 부분을 구성하기 때문에, 사람들이 **훈련**을 받지 않고 자신의 문화양식을 설명하는 것은 어려운 일이다. 언어를 제대로 학습하지 않은 원어민이 종종 문법구조를 설명하는 데 많은 어려움을 겪는 것처럼, 문화를 학습할 줄 모르는 특정 문화의 구성원들은 문화의 구성요소를 설명하고 이러한 요소들이 어떻게 세상에 대한 사람들의 관점과 판단을 형성하는가를 이해하는 데 어려움을 겪는다.

▶ 이종현T의 Logical Point

빈칸 뒷 내용을 보면 문화를 학습할 줄 모르면 이해를 어려워한다는 내용이 나와 있으므로 학습의 내용이 빈칸에 들어가야 한다. 따라서 정답은 (B)가 된다.

24. 정답 : (A)

▶ 해석 : 몇몇 인기있는 음식들은 너무나도 많은 **다양성**을 지니고 있어서 심지어 같은 도시에 있는 사람들도 그들이 어떻게 만들어져야하는지에 대해서 동의할 수 없다.

▶ 이종현T의 Logical Point

that절의 결과 내용이 같은 지역 사람들도 준비하는 방법에 동의할 수 없다는 것이므로 그정도로 많다는 것을 추론할 수 있다. 따라서 정답은 (A)가 된다.

25. 정답 : (A)

▶ 해석 : 도킨스(Dawkins)는 유기체(생명체)는 **반격하는** 경향이 있기 때문에 바위나 강과는 다르다는 점을 지적하고 있다. 진화해서 폭력적으로 된 생명체는 다른 구성원이 대체로 진화해서 마찬가지로 폭력적으로 된 종의 한 구성원이다. 만약 당신이 당신과 같은 종의 한 구성원을 공격한다면 그 상대방은 당신만큼 이나 강하고 공격적일지도 모르고 당신과 똑같은 무기와 방어책으로 무장되어 있을지도 모른다. 다신이 당신과 같은 종의 한 구성원을 공격할 때 당신이 다칠 수 있는 가능성은 무차별적인 공격을 선호하지 않도록 하는 강력한 선택 압력이다. 그것은 또한 보통 사람들이 제시하는 폭력에 관한 대부분의 설명(이론) – 가령 피의 갈증, 죽음에 대한 동경, 살인 본능, 그리고 다른 파괴적인 욕망, 욕구 그리고 충동 –을 배제시킨다. 폭력 성향이 발달될 때 그것은 항상 **전략적인** 것이다.

▶ 이종현T의 Logical Point

첫번째 빈칸 다음 문장을 보면 다른 종들이 폭력적이 되어서 자기도 폭력적이 되었다는 내용이므로 수준을 맞추고 갚아주거나 혹은 다른 것들을 따라한다는 내용이 들어가야 한다. 그리고 두번째 빈칸 앞부분을 보면 그렇다고 해서 무차별적인 공격을 선호하는 방법으로는 안간다고 되어 있으므로 적절하게 조절한다는 것을 알 수 있다. 따라서 두번째 빈칸에는 전략적인 같은 표현이 필요하다. 그래서 정답은 (A)가 된다.

26. 정답 : (B)

▶ 해석 : 평균 온도가 매우 느리게 증가할 때, 정상적인 기초 상태와의 차이점을 알아차리는 것이 어렵게 된다. 왜냐하면 그 변화는 거의 **인식할 수 없기** 때문이다.

▶ 이종현T의 Logical Point

온도가 매우 느리게 증가해서 변화를 알아차리기가 어렵다는 내용이 나와 있다 따라서 빈칸에도 알아차리기 어렵다는 내용이 필요하고 정답은 (B)가 된다.

27. 정답 : (B)

▶ 해석 : Mary Wollstonecraft의 여성 평등에 대한 **지지**는 그녀의 글들이 초기 여성 운동에 매우 형력을 미치게 했다.

▶ 이종현T의 Logical Point

초기 여성 운동에 많은 영향을 준 것이므로 여성 평등을 적극적으로 했다는 것을 알 수 있다. 따라서 정답은 (B)가 된다.

28. 정답 : (A)

▶ 해석 : 오늘날 미국 문화를 연구하는 사람들이 고전음악을 무시하는 경향이 있음은 이해할 만하다. 우리 시대에서는 미국의 음악적 고급문화가 현재 시대와 동떨어진 정형화된 오락으로 전락하고 말았다. 그러므로 우리 오케스트라들이 몰두하고 있는 것들을 놓친다고 하더라도 이는 그리 큰 **희생**이 아니다. 그러나 도금시대 후기에는, 음악이 "예술의 여왕"으로 널리 존경받았다. 고전 음악은 그때가 미국에서의 전성기로서 문화 전반의 중심에 자리 잡고 있었다.

▶ 이종현T의 Logical Point

however을 기준으로 앞 뒤가 대조가 되는 글의 구조를 취하고 있다. however 뒷내용은 클레식 음악이 굉장히 인정받는다는 내용이므로 앞 내용은 인정 못받는다는 얘기가 된다. 따라서 오케스트라가 뭘 하고 있는지를 모르는 것은 당연하다는 의미가 필요하다. 그래서 정답은 (A)가 된다. 그걸 모르는 것이 큰 걸 희생하는 것은 아니라는 의미가 된다.

29. 정답 : (B)

▶ 해석 : Mojave Desert의 경계선은 일반적으로 Yucca brevifolia의 존재에 의해 **경계가 구별되어졌다**. 그 지역에 대한 상징적인 존재이다.

이종현T의 Logical Point

경계선에 관련된 얘기이므로 그와 비슷한 내용의 단어가 필요하다. 따라서 정답은 (B)가 된다.

30. 정답 : (D)

해석 : Mrs. Amherst는 너무나도 예민하고 **안목이 있는** 도서관 사서여서 그녀는 어떤 책이 각각의 학생들에게 적합할지를 정확하게 아는 능력이 있었다.

이종현T의 Logical Point

that절 뒤의 이야기가 학생들에게 적합한 책을 안다는 얘기이므로 그와 관련된 표현이 빈칸에 들어가야 한다. 따라서 정답은 (D)가 된다.

31. 정답 : (D)

해석 : 현재의 경제적 상황 하에서는 요령 있는 구직 희망자라면 미래의 고용주에게 자신의 **신뢰성**을 증명해 보이기 위해 어떤 자리에서든 적어도 1년 동안의 경험을 갖춰야 한다고 상정하는 것이 일반화 되었다. 사실, 이런 주장을 하는 이들은 대중매체에 본질적으로 자축 분위기의 자기 잇속만 차리는 글들을 쓰면서 서로를 인용한다. **그러나** 이런 소위 전문가들은 그러고 나서 구직 희망자의 이력서에서 1년 미만 지속된 일자리들은 빼라고 제안함으로써 자신들의 전문성이 결여되어 있음을 종종 스스로 노출시킨다.

이종현T의 Logical Point

미래의 사장님들에게 자신의 능력을 증명한다는 얘기가 첫번째 빈칸에는 필요하다. 그리고 두번째 빈칸 앞에는 서로를 인용한다고 되어 있고 빈칸 뒤에는 스스로 전문성이 결여되어 있음을 노출시킨다는 안 좋은 이야기가 있으므로 역접의 연결사가 필요하다. 따라서 정답은 (D)가 된다.

32. 정답 : (A)

해석 : 지지율을 **끌어올리기** 위해, 그 현직자는 최근에 일자리 창출에서 이뤄낸 진척에 관한 **찬사**들을 언론매체에 대대적으로 보내라고 당내 충성파들에게 지시했다.

이종현T의 Logical Point

일자리 창출에 대한 최근의 개발에 대한 것이므로 좋은 내용이다. 따라서 각 빈칸에는 전부 좋은 내용이 필요하다. 그랬을 때 정답은 (A)가 된다.

33. 정답 : (B)

해석 : 생물의 색깔은 은폐(발견을 피하는 능력), 의사소통, 체온조절을 비롯한 수많은 생태적 환경 속에서 **적응적** 기능을 할 수 있다. 그러한 것으로서 생물의 색깔은 다양하고 서로 경쟁적인 요구들 간의 균형을 반영할 가능성이 높다. 하나의 기능(예를 들어, 포식자를 피하는 것)을 수행하는 데 가장 적합한 색깔이 또 다른 기능(예를 들어, 잠재적 배우자를 유혹하는 것)에 적합한 색깔과 상충관계를 보일 수 있다. 이러한 상충관계는 그 생물이 처한 자연환경 속에서 이용 가능한 빛의 파장에 의해 한층 더 심화된다. 어떤 환경에서 **은폐적인** 색깔 패턴이 다른 환경에서는 눈에 두드러져 보일 수 있다. 다시 말해, 색깔 신호의 상대적 강도는 수용자의 시각체계에 좌우될 뿐만 아니라 색깔 신호가 전달되는 주변 환경 및 매체에도 좌우된다.

이종현T의 Logical Point

두번째 빈칸이 핵심이다. 다른 쪽에서는 두드러진다고 했으므로 한 쪽은 그 반대인 애매하고 숨겨진다는 의미가 와야 한다. 그리고 생물의 색깔이 환경에 반응한다는 내용이므로 적응한다는 adaptive가 첫번째 빈칸에 들어가서 정답은 (B)가 된다.

34. 정답 : (A)

해석 : 릭(Rick)은 간식을 만들고 있다는 사실을 여동생이 아는 것을 원치 않았기 때문에 팝콘 냄새가 위층으로 **퍼져나가지** 않도록 부엌문을 닫았다.

이종현T의 Logical Point

동생이 아는 것을 원하지 않는 것이므로 냄새가 전달되지 못한다는 의미가 들어가야 한다. 따라서 정답은 (A)가 된다.

35. 정답 : (B)

해석 : 사람들은 자신이 행동하는 대로 된다. 사람들이 태도와 특성을 어떻게 습득하는지에 대한 이와 같은 설명은 작고한 영국 철학자 길버트 라일(Gibert Ryle)까지 거슬러 올라가지만 사회 심리학자 데릴 벰(Daryl Bem)의 자기지각 이론에서 공식화되었다. 벰은 사람들은 자신의 행동을 관찰함으로써 자신이 누구인지에 관한 추론을 이끌어낸다고 주장한다. 자기지각 이론은 상식을 완전히 뒤집는다. 사람들은 그들의 성격적 특성과 태도 때문에 특정한 방식으로 행동한다. 그렇지 않은가? 사람들은 자신이 정직하기 때문에 주운 지갑을 되돌려주고, 환경을 걱정하기 때문에 쓰레기를 재활용한다. **행동은 우리의 내면적 성향에서 우러나온다**는 것은 자명하지만, 벰의 통찰은 그 반대 역시 사실이라는 것을 시사한다. 우리가 주운 지갑을 되돌려준다면 그로 인해 우리의 정직 지수는 한 눈금 높아진다. 재활용품 용기를 길가까지 끌어놓고 나면, 우리는 자신이 정말 환경을 염려한다고 추론하게 되는 것이다.

이종현T의 Logical Point

빈칸 앞을 보면 성격적 특성과 태도 때문에 행동한다는 얘기가 나온다. 이와 같은 얘기가 빈칸에 들어가야 하므로 정답은 (B)가 된다.

36. 정답 : (A)

해석 : 나는 상인과 물건 값에 대해 **흥정을 할** 때마다 내가 산 물건들에 대해 정당한 가격을 지불했는지 확신이 서지 않기 때문에, 정찰제를 시행하는 가게에서 쇼핑하기를 선호한다.

이종현T의 Logical Point

정찰제를 시행하는 가게를 선호한다는 것이므로 그와 반대되는 가격이 조절되는 것을 싫어한다는 것을 알 수 있다. 따라서 정답은 (A)가 된다.

37. 정답 : (D)

해석 : 기생 식물들은 태양 에너지로부터 직접 양분을 생산하기보다는 숙주 식물들이 생산한 양분을 활용함으로써 생존하는 식물들이다. 생존하기 위해 햇빛을 필요로 하지 않기 때문에, 기생 식물들은 햇빛에 직접 노출된 지역보다는 **그늘진** 지역에서 일반적으로 발견된다. 기생 식물들은 흡수근이라는 뿌리를 이용해 주로 숙주 식물의 줄기나 뿌리에 둘러붙는다. 기생식물들은 숙주 식물의 양분 통로 속으로 자신의 흡수근을 뻗어 자신의 생존에 필요한 양분을 숙주 식물로부터 흡수한다. 세상에서 가장 무거운 꽃인 라플레시아(rafflesia)는 밀림의 덩굴 식물들의 뿌리에 의지해 살아가는 기생 식물이다. 이 **육중한** 꽃의 무게는 15파운드까지 나가고 폭이 3피트까지 이르기도 한다.

이종현T의 Logical Point

첫번째 빈칸에는 rather than으로 연결되어 있으니 햇빛에 직접 노출되는 것과 반대되는 얘기가 와야 한다. 따라서 햇빛을 받지 않는다는 얘기가 필요하고, 두번째 빈칸에는 무게와 관련된 내용이 와야 하므로 정답은 (D)가 된다.

38. 정답 : (D)

해석 : 그는 자신의 직무를 수행하는 데 **성실하였으므로**, 그의 고용주들은 그의 업무에 불만을 제기할 수 없었다.

이종현T의 Logical Point

불만을 제기할 수 없다는 것과 같은 맥락이 필요하므로 정답은 (D)가 된다.

39. 정답 : (B)

해석 : 정부의 지출 삭감과 높은 이자율이 지속되면서 인플레이션은 **잦아들었지만**, 그러한 '치료법'은 1979년 이래 겪고 있었던 경기후퇴를 **가속화시켰고**, 1930년대 이래 최악의 경기침체를 불러왔다. 공장들이 문을 닫았고, 기업들이 도산했으며, 담보대출을 갚지 못한 농장들의 압류 비율은 점점 높아졌다. 1982년 말에는 이미 1,200만 명 이상의 미국인들이 실직 상태였는데, 이는 전체 노동력의 10퍼센트 이상에 달하는 규모였다. 두 자릿수 인플레이션은 두 자리 수 실업이라는 대가를 치르고 종식되었던 것이다.

이종현T의 Logical Point

두번째 줄에서 the 'cure'에 해당하는 것이 앞 문장 내용이다. 따라서 인플레이션은 줄었다는 얘기가 필요하다. 그런데 but으로 역접이 되어 있으니 또 다른 문제가 나옴을 알 수 있다. 따라서 가속화시킨다는 정답은 (B)가 된다.

40. 정답 : (A)

해석 : **항성에 대한** 연구는 그 새로운 망원경에 의해 크게 발전했다.

이종현T의 Logical Point

망원경과 관련된 연구가 되므로 정답은 (A)가 된다.

41. 정답 : (A)

해석 : 아리스토텔레스(Aristotle)는 용어에 사물의 본질의 이름이 정의돼 있는 것으로 간주하고, (용어를) 정의하는 공식을 그 본질에 대한 기술로 간주한다. 그리고 그는 정의하는 공식은 문제의 사물의 본질 내지는 본질적 특성들을 **철저하게 기술**해야 한다고 주장한다. 따라서 "강아지는 발이 4개이다."라는 진술은 비록 사실이라고 해도, 만족스런 정의는 아닌 것이다. 왜냐하면 그것은 강아지다움의 본질과 관련된 모든 특징을 포함하고 있지 못하며, 말(馬)에게도 적용될 수 있기 때문이다. 이와 마찬가지로 "강아지는 갈색이다."라는 진술도 강아지 몇 마리에게는 적용될 수 있지만, 모든 강아지에게 적용되는 것은 아니다. 그리고 그 진술은 정의하는 용어의 본질이 아니라 단지 부수적인 속성만을 기술하고 있는 것이다.

이종현T의 Logical Point

빈칸 뒷 내용을 보면 모든 것들에 적용 가능하게 기술하라고 되어 있다. 즉 꼼꼼하게 기술하라는 내용이 와야 함을 알 수 있고 정답은 (A)가 된다.

42. 정답 : (B)

해석 : 마다가스카르 섬에 서식하고 있는 아이아이(aye-aye) 원숭이는 전 세계에서 가장 회귀한 영장류 가운데 하나이다. 이들의 가장 주목할 만한 특징은 기다란 중지(中指)인데, 아이아이 원숭이는 이 중지를 이용해서 나무에 사는 곤충유충과 과일의 과육을 파먹는다. 먹이를 찾는 과정에서 아이아이 원숭이는 나무의 표면을 가볍게 두드려 **비어 있는 곳을 알아낸 뒤에** 그 내용물을 판단한다. 그리고 날카로운 앞니로 나무의 부드러운 부분을 물어 뜯어내어 통로를 낸 다음, 기다란 중지를 밀어 넣어 포획한 유충을 꺼낸다. 아이아이 새끼 원숭이는 호기심 많은 손가락으로 곤충 유충을 찾아서 꺼내는 방법을 어렸을 때 엄마 원숭이로부터 배운다. 처음에는 찾은 것마다 전부 두들겨 대며 서툴기 짝이 없지만, 경험이 쌓여가면서는 **아주 빠른 속도로 능숙해진다**.

이종현T의 Logical Point

나무에서 파먹는다는 내용이므로 첫번째 빈칸에는 음식을 찾는다는 내용이 필요하다. 그리고 두번째 빈칸에는 처음에는 서툴지만 나중에는 능숙해진다는 내용이 필요하다. 따라서 정답은 (B)가 된다.

43. 정답 : (D)

해석 : 위조범들은 그림에 금이 가도록 열을 가하는 것을 포함해서 그림이 그려진 시기를 **조작하기** 위해 무엇이든 할 수 있다.

이종현T의 Logical Point

위조자들이 하는 행동에 대한 내용이므로 정답은 (D)가 된다.

UNIT 2 재진술과 부연설명

예 시 문 제

1. 정답 : (E)

해석 : 그녀는 시장이 그의 선거 캠페인동안의 약속을 **포기하는** 것처럼 느껴서 그 시장의 정책에 어안이 벙벙해졌다.

이종현T의 Logical Point

시장이 캠페인동안의 약속을 '빈칸'해서 그 시장의 지금 정책에 어안이 벙벙해졌다는 내용이다. 지금 시장의 정책에 어안이 벙벙해지는 것은 시장의 정책을 예측하지 못했다는 것이고 그가 했던 약속과는 다르다는 의미의 내용이 들어와야 하기 때문에 정답은 (E) abjured가 된다.

2. 정답 : (E)

해석 : Jen이 그녀의 매니저의 조카가 그녀 위로 승진했다는 것을 알게 되었을 때, 그녀는 회사가 **친족 등용**을 한다고 주장하면서 격분했다.

이종현T의 Logical Point

매니저의 조카가 그녀보다 더 높이 승진하게 되었다는 내용이 계속 들어가야 한다. 조카가 승진한 것과 가장 깊은 단어가 nepotism이므로 정답은 (E)가 된다.

3. 정답 : (B)

해석 : 지식 사회는 소련의 몰락을 예측하지 못한 것에 대해서 **비난 받아서는** 안 된다. 심지어 Hedrick Smith조차도 1986년도에 소련은 가장 안정적인 사회라고 말했다.

이종현T의 Logical Point

지식 사회의 대표적인 인물이 Hedrick Smith라는 것을 보고 두 개가 같은 표현이라는 것을 보는 것이 핵심이다. 그래서 심지어 대표적인 인물이 이 사람도 예측하지 못했다는 내용이 뒤에 나와있다. 따라서 예측하지 못한 것은 잘못이 아니다는 내용이 들어가야 하므로 정답은 (B)가 된다.

4. 정답 : (B)

해석 : **변덕스러운** 가수는 종종 콘서트를 슬픈 분위기로 시작해서, 중간엔 화를 내고, 그리고 마지막엔 가능한 한 행복한 상태로 돌아온다.

이종현T의 Logical Point

뒷 내용을 보면 슬픈 분위기, 화를 내는 분위기, 행복한 분위기 등의 여러 분위기가 나온다. 그러니 가수는 여러 다양한 감정을 느끼는 내용이므로 다양한의 의미를 담을 수 있는 (B) mercurial(변덕스러운)이 정답이다.

5. 정답 : (A)

해석 : Hume의 계승자들 사이에선, 온전한 정신상태라는 것은 피상적임을 의미해왔다, 그리고 **심오함**이라는 것은 어느정도의 미침을 의미해왔다.

이종현T의 Logical Point

지문에서 sanity와 뒷 문장의 some degree of madness가 반대되는 의미를 지니고 있다. 그러므로 빈칸에는 첫 문장의 목적어의 반대가 오는 것이 좋다. 따라서 superficiality의 반대인 정답은 (A) profundity가 된다.

6. 정답 : (D)

해석 : **측근 봐주기**와 부패가 그 나라 전체를 송두리째 파먹고 있다. 모든 수준의 정부 **조달**사업은 현재 뇌물 수수로 가득하다. 비정부기구인 부패파수꾼은 학교 계좌에서 현금을 빼돌리는 **부정한** 학교 교장들과 관련된 신고를 1,000건 이상 받았다고 한다.

이종현T의 Logical Point

첫번째 빈칸엔 corruption(부패)와 비슷한 의미와 느낌의 단어가 들어가야 한다. 그리고 세 번째 빈칸에서도 '빈칸'한 학교 교장이라고 나오는데 그 학교 교장은 학교 계좌에서 돈을 훔친 교장이므로 좋지 않은 교장이 되어야 한다. 그랬을 때 정답이 될 수 있는 것은 (D)가 된다.

7. 정답 : (B)

해석 : Hammerhead 상어들은 음성 부력이 가장 강력하고 또한 부분적으로 **다른 종들의 입들**에 비해 작은 입술을 가지고 있다.

이종현T의 Logical Point

문법 문제에 해당한다. 지금은 small mouths와 다른 상어들의 mouth들을 비교하는 것이므로 복수인 those를 써서 those of other species가 와야 하므로 정답은 (B)가 된다.

8. 정답 : (A)

해석 : '정치적인 이유로 제한된' 이라는 표현은 정부가 인식하기에 당혹스럽거나 위협적인 정보를 시민들이 받지 못하게 막는 **고압적인** 정부라는 이미지를 준다.

➡ 이종현T의 Logical Point

정부가 인식하기에 시민들이 위협감을 느끼고 당황할 수 있는 정보들은 얻지 못하게 막는 정부라는 내용이 빈칸에 들어가야 한다. 그래서 굉장히 억압적인의 의미가 되는 (A) heavy-handed가 된다. (D)의 솔직히 말하지 않는 정부가 매력적인 오답이지만 여기서 정부가 거짓말하고 있다는 얘기는 나오고 있지 않으므로 정답은 (A)로 가는 것이 맞다.

9. 정답 : (A)

➡ 해석 : 우리는 오늘날 여러 가지 밈(비유전적 문화 요소)에 몰두해 있다. 이것들은 어린 시절에 형성되는, 새로운 정보와 영향력에 대한 인간 정신의 수용성을 이용하여 모방 및 선천적으로 **쉽게 믿어버리는 성향**에 의해 확산된다. 여기서는 무비판적인 모방이 선호된다. 사람들은 **싫든 좋든 간에** 뭔가를 습득할 수밖에 없다.

➡ 이종현T의 Logical Point

첫번째 빈칸에는 모방하는 것과 비슷한 느낌의 단어가 와야 한다. 근데 그것은 새로운 정보에 대한 인간 정신의 수용성에 대한 것이므로 받아들인다는 의미의 credulity가 들어가야 한다. 그리고 두번째 빈칸에서는 문장의 의미가 무조건 무엇인가는 생긴다는 의미이므로 무조건이 될 수 있는 의미의 willy-nilly가 들어가서 정답은 (A)가 된다.

10. 정답 : (B)

➡ 해석 : 사람들은 유아기 경험이 특정한 패턴을 확립하고 여러 요인들을 작동시킨다는 것을 믿고, 나머지 아동기 동안에, 아이들은 이러한 초기 특징들의 **결과**에 대처해야 한다고 믿는다.

➡ 이종현T의 Logical Point

아동기는 유아기 이후에 발생되는 것이므로 아이들이 해야할 것은 유아기 때 확립된 패턴을 다룬다는 내용이므로 빈칸에는 (B) upshot이 들어가야 한다.

11. 정답 : (D)

➡ 해석 : 우리가 먹은 음식값을 지불하고 우리의 신체활동들을 체크해주는 스마트워치의 능력이 가능한 것은 그 작은 금속몸체 안에 가득 채워져 있는 무수히 많은 센서들 덕분이다. 그러나 이 정교한 센서들은 조금씩 당신의 디지털 **프라이버시**를 갉아먹고 있다. 이러한 부작용 이면의 기본적인 주된 요인은 지능적으로 키보드조작을 추적하는 프로그램이 사람들의 타이핑 습관들로부터 만들어진 행동주의적 생물 통계학 프로필들에 기초하여 개인들을 인지할 수 있는 것과 유사한 방식이다. 사람들이 공간 속으로 손을 움직이는 모습은, 사람마다 조금씩 다른 한, 이론적으

로는, 개인 성격 등을 알아내기 위해 탐색될 수 있고, 개인의 접속정보를 훼손하려는 더욱 지능적인 시도에 사용될 수도 있다. **설상가상으로** 대부분의 키보드와 핀 패드들은 크기가 표준화되어 사용자들이 사용 중에 더욱 편하게 느끼게 해준다.

이종현T의 Logical Point

첫번째 빈칸을 가지도 두번째 빈칸은 끼워맞춰야 한다. 첫번째 빈칸을 보면, 빈칸 다음 문장에서 this side effect라는 표현이 있으므로 앞 문장에 chipping away your digital '빈칸'은 부정적인 부작용이 되는 것이다. 그리고 뒤의 내용은 타이핑을 바탕으로 그 개인을 인지할 수 있다는 내용이므로 그 사람이 누군지 파고들 수 있다는 privacy가 정답에 적절하다. 두번째 빈칸은 사람들이 표준화된 키보드를 보며 더 편하게 잘 사용하므로 더 잘 알아볼 수 있다는 의미가 강화가 되어서 정답은 What is worse가 되고 (D)가 된다.

12. 정답 : (D)

해석 : 서양의 가장 초기 예술 이론은 예술은 현실의 **모사**인 모방이라고 제안했다.

이종현T의 Logical Point

동격의 문제이다. 즉 mimesis의 동격의 의미가 빈칸에 와야 한다. 따라서 답이 될 수 있는 (D) semblance가 정답이다.

13. 정답 : (E)

해석 : 유전 치료학자들이 유적적인 뇌 질병을 치료하는 것을 도울지도 모르는 한 바이러스는 치료하는 바이러스를 직접적으로 머리에 주사할 필요성을 **제거하면서** 말초 신경 시스템으로 들어가서 머리로 이동할 수 있다.

이종현T의 Logical Point

지문에서 enter ~ brain과 inject the ~ virus directly into the brain 이 부분이 대조가 된다. 따라서 앞의 주절의 바이러스가 생겨났으니 대조가 되는 분사구문의 목적어는 없어지는 것이다. 그래서 없어지는 의미의 정답은 (E)가 된다.

14. 정답 : (B)

해석 : 그러나 윌슨(Wilson)이 말하듯이, 자유 의지에 대한 우리의 **완강한** 고집은 일종의 진화적 의미가 있다. 사실, 인간이 지닌 **가장 강력한** 진화적 장점은 집단적 의미를 창출하려는 인간의 본능적 욕구였다. 이러한 욕구는 가차 없는 만큼 창의적인 것이기도 해서 절망, 우울, 참사, 집단 학살, 전쟁, 재난, 전염병, 심지어 과학의 굴욕들을 이해할 수 있는 길을 찾아줄 수 있다.

이종현T의 Logical Point

이 문제는 선지에서 같은 속성의 선지를 찾아서 연결시켜보는 것이 중요한 문제이다. (B)를 보면 첫번째 빈칸에 dogged를 넣으면 완강한 고집이 된다. 완강한 고집이 되면 정말 그렇게만 할려고 하는 것이므로 두번째 빈칸에 keenest가 들어갔을 때 가장 강렬하게 원하는 진화적인 이점이 되어서 같은 의미가 된다. 따라서 정답은 (B)가 된다.

15. 정답 : (A)

해석 : 순록은 툰드라에서 거대한 울타리 안으로 **보살펴져 들어올** 때까지 개별적으로 자유로이 살아간다. 양치기와 다른 주인들은 이따금씩 올가미로 한 마리씩 끄집어내면서 오랫동안 순록들을 지켜보며 서 있다. 순록들은 귀에 칼로 무늬를 새겨 표시하는데, 이것은 주인마다 서로 다르다. 양치기들은 빠르게 움직이고 있는 순록들의 몸에 있는 표시를 먼 거리에서 볼 수 있는 **신비한** 능력을 가지고 있다. 나는 수천 마리의 순록들이 진흙 묻은 울타리 주위를 돌고 있는 모습에 매료된 채로 담장에 기대어 서 있는데, 뿔과 진흙과 발굽들이 흐릿한 모습이다.

이종현T의 Logical Point

첫번째 빈칸을 보면 ~할 때까지 자유롭게 산다고 되어 있다. 그럼 단순하게 생각하면 자유로워지지 않을 때 까지 자유롭게 산다는 내용이고 어떤 것들의 안으로 들어간다는 내용인 wrangled가 오면 적절하다. 그리고 먼 거리에서 순록들의 표시를 볼 수 있는 능력이므로 대단한 능력과 비슷한 uncanny가 와서 정답은 (A)가 된다.

16. 정답 : (C)

해석 : 북아프리카와 중동 전역에서 벌어지고 있는 극적인 사건에서, 모로코는 다소 각본에서 벗어나고 있다. 수만 명의 사람들이 부패를 비난하고 민주적인 개혁을 요구하면서 전국적으로 가두행진을 벌였지만, 통치자인 '무하마드 6세(Mohammad VI)'의 축출을 요구하는 사람은 거의 없었다. 그 군주는 모로코에 안정과 번영을 가져다준 공로를 인정받는 **인기가 많은** 인물이다.

이종현T의 Logical Point

빈칸 앞 문장을 보면 무하마드 6세의 축출을 요구하는 사람이 없다고 나와 있다. 즉 인기 많은 사람이고 빈칸에도 좋은 의미가 들어간다는 것을 알 수 있다. 따라서 정답은 (C)가 된다.

17. 정답 : (B)

해석 : 사회 역사의 본질과 서정시는 <u>**현저하게 대조를 이룬다**</u>. 사회과학은 항상 <u>**덧없는 것**</u>들을 이야기하고 서정시는 패션과 경제를 너머 영원한 본질인 변하지 않는 인간의 본질에 대해 이야기한다.

이종현T의 Logical Point

social history와 lyric poetry는 같은 것일 수도 있고 대조되는 개념일 수도 있다고 접근을 해야한다. 그랬을 때 뒤의 두번째 빈칸에서 the 뒤의 빈칸이 변하지 않는 인간의 본질에 대한 내용이면 두 개는 같은것이고 반대되는 것이면 대조되는 것이다. 여기선 같은 의미를 만들어주는 단어가 없으므로 반대로 보면 되고 정답은 (B)가 된다.

18. 정답 : (E)

해석 : 원래, 대중문화의 가장 지적인 비평은, 본성적으로 <u>**부정적**</u>이다. 호소하는 곳이 더 넓어질수록 제품이 더 <u>**조잡해진다는**</u> 가정에 기초하기 때문이다.

이종현T의 Logical Point

분사구문으로 이어지기 때문에 기본적으로 같은 문장이다. 그래서 둘 다 긍정과 둘 다 부정의 개념으로 접근을 한다. 그랬을 때 정답은 (E)가 된다.

19. 정답 : (E)

해석 : 드론이 한 사물을 바라볼 때, 그 사물은 흔히 목표물처럼 보이기 마련이다. 사람들은 사격 범위에 들어 있는 그림자가 된다. 건물은 공격받기 쉬워 보이는데, 건물의 지붕이 속수무책으로 노출되어 무방비 상태에 놓여 있기 때문이다. 대부분의 색은 사라지고, 남아 있는 검은색, 흰색, 회색은 그 장면에서 모든 인간의 의미를 빼앗는다. 우리가 보는 것은 사망자 집계와, 피해 보도와, 전략적 가치 등과 같은 <u>**자료**</u>가 된다.

이종현T의 Logical Point

body counts, damage reports 등을 일반화 시킬 수 있는 동격의 표현은 (E)가 된다.

20. 정답 : (B)

해석 : 미래 세대들은 우주에서 인류의 위치에 대한 현재의 추론들을 생략과 실수에 의해 망쳐진다고 여긴다: 심지어 엄격한 과학적인 관점들조차도 밤시간 동안에 때때로 바뀐다.

이종현T의 Logical Point

빈칸에는 안좋은 얘기가 들어가야 한다. 빈칸 뒤의 단어가 안좋기 때문이다. 그렇기 때문에 정답은 (B)가 된다.

21. 정답 : (B)

해석 : 아직 눈이 뜨지 못한 매니저들은 거의 심각한 갈등의 수준에 대한 중요한 이유를 인식하지 못한다. 민주적으로 운영되는 그룹들 사이에서. 그리고 약간의 관용은 종종 <u>**갈등**</u>을 막아준다.

이종현T의 Logical Point

갈등과 비슷한 얘기가 빈칸에 들어가야 한다. 따라서 정답은 (B) schism이다.

22. 정답 : (D)

해석 : Marshall의 대립을 일삼는 스타일은 거의 어느 누구라도 멀어지게 만들 수 있다. 그리고 그는 심지어 수많은 그의 지지자들을 포함하고 쉽게 <u>**화나지 않는다는**</u> 평판을 가진 임원진들의 적대감을 불러일으켰다.

이종현T의 Logical Point

쉽게 '빈칸'하지 않는 사람들도 적대감이 들게 한다고 했으므로 화나게 하는 사람의 의미가 들어가야 한다. 따라서 정답은 (D)가 된다.

23. 정답 : (B)

해석 : 문장에서 단어의 순서는 현재 프랑스어보다 과거 프랑스어에서 훨씬 더 자유로웠다. 이 <u>**자유**</u>는 프랑스어가 점차적으로 그 뚜렷한 점을 잃어버리가 시작하면서 사라졌다.

이종현T의 Logical Point

앞/뒤가 같은 문장이 되어야 하므로 this가 가리키는 것이 Old French라는 것을 알면 자유롭다는 말이 들어가야 한다. 따라서 정답은 (B)가 된다.

24. 정답 : (C)

해석 : <u>**이동성**</u>은 중요하다. 운전할 권리를 잃는 것은 많은 노인들에게 있어 배우자를 잃는 것만큼이나 큰 충격을 준다. 또한, 인구가 고령화되어 감에 따라, 미래에 더 많은 사람들이 그 충격을 느끼게 될 것이다. 그러나 나이가 많은 운전자 자신의 안전은 말할 것도 없고, 다른 도로 이용자들의 안전이 가장 중요하다.

이종현T의 Logical Point

바로 다음 문장에 운전하는 권한을 잃는 것은 과부가 되는 정도로 대단히 충격적이라고 되어 있다. 따라서 그 운전하는 권한은 굉장히 중요하다고 추론 가능하다. 이와 관련된 선지는 (C)가 된다.

25. 정답 : (A)

해석 : Robin의 말은 감정과 관련이 있었다. 그들은 오로지 임박한 극단적인 감정들에 대한 신중한 **제한, 균형**에 의해 그들의 안정된 톤을 유지했다.

이종현T의 Logical Point

level과 extreme이 역접이 된다. 즉 극단적인 것들을 어떻게 해서 안정적인 톤을 유지해야 한다. 따라서 정답은 (D)가 되는 것이 좋다. 다만 여러 감정들과 균형을 맞춘다는 의미가 되기 때문에 (A)도 괜찮다.

26. 정답 : (D)

해석 : Mac Rory의 대화는 **지루했다**. 그녀는 하나의 이야기도 할 수 없었다. 그녀는 항상 이야기를 까먹었기 때문이다. 그리고 그녀는 절대 재치있는 말을 하지 못했다. 우연이 아니라면.

이종현T의 Logical Point

항상 까먹어서 어떤 이야기를 할 수 없다고 되어 있고 재치있는 말도 절대 하지 못했단 내용이 : 뒤에 나와 있으므로 빈칸에도 재미없다는 내용이 들어간다. 따라서 정답은 (D)가 된다.

27. 정답 : (C)

해석 : 캐릭터들 사이에 신랄한 단어들을 주고받는 대화는 그 소설을 **생동감 있게** 읽게 해 준다. 그리고 이러한 매우 **활발함**은 나에게 그 의견들 중 몇몇은 작가의 의견일 수도 있다는 것을 시사한다.

이종현T의 Logical Point

첫번째 문장에서 목적격 보어와, 뒷 문장의 주어가 같다고 보고 두 빈칸에는 같은 내용이 들어간다고 보면 정답은 (C)가 된다

28. 정답 : (C)

해석 : 겜블러들이 성공하지 않는 전략을 **유지**하는 것은 환상에 대한 **기능**이다. 그리고 이 기능은 플레이어들을 잘못 이끌어서 그들의 돈을 가져가기 위해 그 도박에 내재되어 있다.

이종현T의 Logical Point

겜블러들이 성공하지 않는 전략은 플레이어를 속여서 돈을 가져가기 위한 방법이라는 의미가 와야 한다. 따라서 빈칸에는 유지와 기능의 (C)가 정답이 된다.

29. 정답 : (C)

해석 : 수십년동안, 초대칭성에 대한 개념은 현대 물리학에서 가장 큰 **수수께끼들** 중 하나였다. 그리고 이것은 반복적으로 이해하려는 과학자들의 시도를 **좌절시켰다**.

이종현T의 Logical Point

같은 방향으로 가야 한다. 그랬을 때 수수께끼이고 이걸 아직 해결하지 못했다고 될 수 있는 (C)가 정답이 된다.

30. 정답 : (C)

해석 : 몇몇 비평가들은 작가의 인류학에 대한 연구가 그의 문학 스타일에 **영향을 주었다**고 제안했고 정말로, 인류학적인 참고사항들이 종종 그의 작품들에 **뿌려졌다**.

이종현T의 Logical Point

두 빈칸이 같은 방향으로 가야 한다. 인류학 적인 연구와 그의 작품의 관계를 찾는 것이므로 관계가 깊을 수도 있고 아예 없을 수도 있다. 여기서 일단 깊다고 봤을 때 연결될 수 있는 표현이 (C)이므로 정답은 (C)가 된다. inform은 알리다 라는 뜻도 있지만 영향을 미치다 라는 뜻도 있다.

31. 정답 : (D)

해석 : 학문적인 말다툼들로부터 멀리 떨어져서 있는 그 작가는 복잡한 토론들에 대해서 명료하고 **명쾌한** 방식으로 토의할 수 있다. 그리고 이것은 뚜렷하게 내부의 **특수 용어**들로부터 자유롭다.

이종현T의 Logical Point

일단 작가의 토론 방식은 굉장히 명쾌하다는 이야기 이므로 첫번째 빈칸에는 명료하다는 얘기가 들어가야 한다. 그리고 두번째 빈칸에는 of 뒤의 명사가 없어서 명쾌한 것이므로 명쾌해지는 것을 방해하는 요소가 들어가야 한다. 따라서 정답은 (D)가 된다.

32. 정답 : (B)

해석 : 이론적으로 가능한 가장 낮은 절대적인 0도에 대한 탐구는 몇몇 과학자들에겐 이루어질 수 없는 꿈과 **유사하다**.

이종현T의 Logical Point

주어에서 0도는 이론적으로만 가능하고 마지막 부분에 Holy Grail은 이루어질 수 없는 꿈이라는 뜻이기 때문에 둘은 유사하다는 내용이 필요하다. 따라서 정답은 (B)가 된다.

33. 정답 : (C)

해석 : 문학에서 현명한 학생들은 문학 비평에서 쓰이는 용어들이 **악명높게 바꾸기 쉽다는** 것을 안다. 그것들의 의미가 그것들을 사용하는 작가의 전제와 토론 중에 있는 작품의 성격에 따라 바뀔 수 있다는 점에서.

이종현T의 Logical Point

in that 절 뒤에서 의미가 계속 바뀐다고 나와 있으므로 바뀐다는 내용이 빈칸에도 들어가야 한다. 따라서 정답은 (C)가 된다.

34. 정답 : (A)

해석 : 외견상으로 잊혀진 땅에 있는 마을 사람들의 대다수는 **마지못한** 채식주의자들이다. 즉, 그들은 신성한 축제기간 동안에만 오로지 고기를 먹는다, 혹은 그들이 이것을 감당할 여유가 있을 때마다, 그리고 그것은 터무니없게도 높은 가격 때문에, 절대 그럴 일이 없다.

이종현T의 Logical Point

뒷 문장을 보면 가격이 높아서 고기를 살 돈이 없어서 채식주의자가 되었다는 것을 알 수 있다. 따라서 정답은 (A)가 된다.

35. 정답 : (C)

해석 : 'catch-22'라는 구절은 Joseph Heller의 소설인 Catch-22에서 발생되었다. 그리고 그 소설에서 한 군인은 군대로부터 제대할 것을 요청한다 그리고는 **난해한** 설명을 듣는다. 그 설명은 제대의 기준이 미치는 것인데, 그가 미친 전쟁에서 포함되지 않기를 요청하기 때문에 그는 정상임에 틀림이 없고 그러므로 미쳐야 제대를 할 수 있다는 것에 기초해서 제대할 수가 없다는 설명이었다.

이종현T의 Logical Point

미치지 않아서 제대할 수 없다는 그의 요청을 근거로 다시 뒤집고 있으므로 정답은 (C)가 된다.

36. 정답 : (C)

해석 : 게임을 진행해 가는 과정은 게이머의 기대에 부응할 정도로 그럴듯하고 자연스러워야 한다. 다시 말해 자연적 지능이 할 것으로 생각될 만한 진행이어야 한다. 그러므로 게임을 진행해 나아가는 것이 반드시 최대한의 기계적 효율성이나 최단거리에 맞게 최적화된 것은 아니다. 사실상 이러한 목표들은 부차적 이거나 심지어 바람직하지 않은 것으로 여겨진다. 다시 말해, 그 목표들이 감각-정서적 또는 심미적 자질이 결여된 채 비현실적이고 기계적으로만 보이는 이동(게임에서의 수)을 초래할 경우, 그러한 이동 자체가 게이머를 **불안하게 만들고** 게이머의 주의를 흩뜨려, 게임을 다시 하고 싶은 마음이 들지 않게 하거나 게임에 몰입하지 못하게 할 것이다.

▶ **이종현T의 Logical Point**

감각, 정서적 부분이 없다면 게이머의 감정을 고려하지 않는다는 얘기가 되고 그 감정과 관련될 만한 단어가 불안하게 만들다이므로 정답은 (C)가 된다.

37. 정답 : (B)

▶ **해석** : "인간은 자신의 역사를 만든다. 하지만 자신이 원하는 그대로는 아니다."라는 마르크스의 **경구**는 자주 반복되는 격언이 되었다.

▶ **이종현T의 Logical Point**

dictum과 같은 표현이 주어에 들어가면 된다. 따라서 정답은 (B)가 된다.

38. 정답 : (D)

▶ **해석** : 한 편의 소설에서 긴장감을 만들어내는 것은 부분적으로는 구체적인 단어들이 서로 연결되어 이야기의 가시적인 행동을 구성하는 방식이다. 그러나 또한 (이야기에) 암시되어 있는 것은 바로 (이야기에서) **빠뜨려져 있는** 것들이며, 이것은 사물의 평온한 표면 바로 **아래에 있는** 풍경이다.

▶ **이종현T의 Logical Point**

단어가 핵심적인 것이라면 빈칸에는 그 핵심적인 것의 반대인 핵심적이지 않은 것들에 대한 얘기가 된다. 따라서 표면 아래에 있고 고려되지 않는다는 의미가 들어가서 정답은 (D)가 된다.

39. 정답 : (A)

▶ **해석** : 그녀의 **쾌활한** 성격은 연례회의장의 우울한 분위기에 더해지기에 환영할 만한 것이었다.

▶ **이종현T의 Logical Point**

환영할만한 것에 대한 것과 같은 표현이 필요하다. 따라서 정답은 (A)가 된다.

40. 정답 : (B)

▶ **해석** : 자석 나침반의 기원은 **베일에 가려져 있다**. 천연 자석의 자기적 성질을 누가 발견했는지는 알려져 있지 않다. 자석의 끌어당기는 힘을 강철이나 담금질한 철에 **옮겨줄 수 있다는** 사실이나 지리적 방향을 정하는 데 자석을 사용할 수 있다는 사실을 누가 발견했는지도 전혀 알려져 있지 않다. 중국인들이 일찍이 11세기 초에 방향을 나타내는 용도로 자성을 띤 바늘을 최초로 사용했을지도 모른다.

▶ **이종현T의 Logical Point**

아무도 모른다는 내용이 첫번째 빈칸에는 필요하다. 그리고 두번째 빈칸에는 자석 나침반의 역할에 대한 얘기이므로 철에 힘이 부여된다는 얘기가 들어가면 된다. 따라서 정답은 (B)가 된다.

41. **정답 : (A)**

해석 : 다양성은 종종 매우 바람직한 것으로 **홍보되어진다**. 실제로, 전문적인 직업의 맥락에서 우리는 더 다양한 구성원으로 이루어진 팀이 종종 **같은 성질의 구성원으로 이루어진** 팀보다 더 나은 기량을 선보인다는 사실을 알고 있다.

이종현T의 Logical Point

다양성의 좋은 점에 대한 얘기이므로 두번째 빈칸에는 다양하지 않은 그룹이 된다. 따라서 정답은 (A)가 된다.

42. **정답 : (B)**

해석 : 1860년대에 작가 레오 톨스토이(Leo Tolstoy)는 러시아의 툴라(Tula)지역에 가족과 함께 **자리 잡았다**. 편안하게 그곳에 정착해 있는 동안 그는 "전쟁과 평화"를 집필하였다.

이종현T의 Logical Point

;(세미 콜론) 뒤에 거기에 정착을 했다는 얘기가 있으므로 빈칸에도 정착을 했다는 얘기가 필요하다. 따라서 정답은 (B)가 된다.

43. **정답 : (B)**

해석 : 데이비드(David)의 얼굴에 나타난 걱정스러운 표정으로 볼 때, 그의 낭비벽으로 인해 그가 금전적으로 **위태로운** 상황에 처했음이 명백했다.

이종현T의 Logical Point

낭비벽과 관련된 표현이므로 금전적으로 힘든 상황이라는 얘기가 들어가야 한다. 따라서 정답은 (B)가 된다.

44. **정답 : (C)**

해석 : 그 연구에서 수행된 다른 비교들은 루시(Lucy)가 비록 직립보행을 했었더라도, 그녀는 현대인보다는 비효율적으로 걸었으며 그 결과 땅 위에서 먼 거리를 걷는 능력은 **제한되었을** 것이라는 점을 시사한다. 또한, 그녀의 모든 팔다리뼈들은 그녀의 체격에 비해 매우 튼튼하다는 것이 밝혀졌는데, 이는 그녀가 현대인보다는 차라리 현대 침팬지의 그것과 유사한 대단히 튼튼한 근육들을 지녔으리라는 점을 시사한다. 인류의 진화 후기에 나타나는 **근력**의 감소는 신체적 노력의 필요성을 감소시킨 더 나은 기술, 그리고 더 커진 뇌의 신진대사적 요구의 증가와 관련된 것으로 보인다.

이종현T의 Logical Point

비효율적과 연결되는 개념이 첫번째 빈칸에는 필요하고 두번째 빈칸 앞에는 현대인보다는 근력이 많다고 되어 있으므로 현대인들은 근력이 적다는 것이 추론 가능하다. 따라서 정답은 (C)가 된다.

45. 정답 : (D)

해석 : 카버(Carver)는 다른 사람들이 자신의 실험을 재현할 수 있도록 상세하게 기록을 남겼다. 그는 본능보다는 주의 깊은 실험에 더욱 의존하는 철저하고, **빈틈없는** 과학자였다.

이종현T의 Logical Point

주의 깊은 실험에 의존한다는 것과 같은 의미의 내용이 필요하므로 정답은 (D)가 된다.

46. 정답 : (B)

해석 : 많은 온라인 구매자들은 사이버 공간에 조금이라도 흔적을 남기는 것에 대해 **겁을 낸다**. 그들은 자신들에 대한 개인 정보를 노출시키기보다는 차라리 웹페이지 접속을 포기하려 한다.

이종현T의 Logical Point

개인 정보를 노출시키지 않고 차라리 접속을 안한다고 되어 있으므로 싫어하고 꺼린다는 내용이 필요하다. 따라서 정답은 (B)가 된다.

47. 정답 : (C)

해석 : 무당거미는 그들의 복잡한 장식들을 **두드러지게** 만드는 특별할 실을 사용하는데, 장식된 부분들이 더 많은 벌레들을 유인하는 것으로 실험 결과 밝혀졌다.

이종현T의 Logical Point

더 많은 벌레들을 유인하는 것과 비슷한 맥락의 얘기가 필요하므로 두드러진다는 (C)가 정답이 된다.

48. 정답 : (D)

해석 : 그는 쓰러지지 않으려고 술주정뱅이처럼 **휘청거리면서** 비틀대고 흔들거렸다.

이종현T의 Logical Point

비틀대고 흔들리는 것과 같은 얘기가 와야 하므로 정답은 (D)가 된다.

49. 정답 : (D)

해석 : **말을 잘하는** 사람인 매튜(Matthew)를 정신과 의사라고 상상하기란 어려웠다. 다른 사람이 말을 하는 동안 듣기만 하는 것은 그의 스타일이 아니었다.

이종현T의 Logical Point

매튜는 다른 사람들이 말을 하는 것들 듣기만 하기를 어려워하는 사람이다. 따라서 본인이 말을 잘하고 많은 사람이라는 것이 추론 가능하고 정답은 (D)가 된다.

50. 정답 : (A)

해석 : 우리는 중립국에 대한 이러한 불법 공격을 **약탈**행위로 간주하며, 그러한 행동을 즉각 중지하고 적절한 반환을 할 것을 요구한다.

이종현T의 Logical Point

반환과 관련된 내용이 와야 하므로 정답은 (A)가 된다.

51. 정답 : (A)

해석 : 내가 말한 그 공무원이 가장 **양심적이었다**. 그는 뇌물을 받기를 거부했고 민원인들이 어려운 일에 처하지 않도록 모든 서류를 꼼꼼하게 검토했기 때문이었다.

이종현T의 Logical Point

뇌물을 받기를 거부하고 모든 서류를 꼼꼼하게 검토하는 것과 관련있는 내용이므로 정답은 (A)가 된다.

52. 정답 : (B)

해석 : **교활한 책략**에 더 능해지면서, 그는 아주 교활하게 정적들을 연이어 공격했다. 그리고 왕좌에 오르는 데 성공했고, 그 왕좌를 유지하기 위해 애썼다.

이종현T의 Logical Point

교활하게 정적들을 공격한다는 것과 관련된 내용이 되어야하므로 정답은 (B)가 된다.

53. 정답 : (B)

해석 : 그 남자의 과거에 대해 많은 부분이 밝혀졌는데, 그것은 모두 **평판이 좋지 않은 것이었다**. 냉혹하고 폭력적인 그의 잔인함에 대한 그의 **비열한** 삶에 대한 그의 이상한 동료들에 대한 그의 경력을 둘러싸고 존대해온 것 같은 증오에 대한 이야기가 들려왔다. 그러나 그의 행방에 대해서는 소문조차 들리지 않았다.

이종현T의 Logical Point

첫번째 빈칸을 보면 좋지 않은 잔인함과 관련되므로 평판이 안좋다는 얘기가 들어가고 두번째 빈칸에도 같은 맥락으로 들어가야 하므로 정답은 (B)가 된다.

54. 정답 : (A)

해석 : 충실한 피그미족 사냥꾼과 함께, 그는 한 무리의 고릴라를 그 고릴라들이 그의 존재를 알아차리지 못할 만큼 충분한 거리를 두고 조심스럽고도 끈덕지게 하루 종일 때로는 며칠간 쫓아다녔다. 이런 **세심한** 추적을 통해, 그는 소심한 영장류 무리를 겁먹게 할 가능성을 **최소화하면서**, 고릴라는 무엇을 먹는지 보금자리는 몇 개를 만드는지 그리고 고릴라 무리의 규모, 나이, 성별에 대해 추론할 수 있는 많은 방법을 배울 수 있었다.

이종현T의 Logical Point

조심스럽고 끈덕지게 추적하므로 그와 관련된 내용이 첫번째 빈칸에 들어간다. 그리고 마찬가지로 같은 맥락의 내용이 두번째 빈칸에도 들어가므로 정답은 (A)가 된다.

55. 정답 : (D)

해석 : 당사자들이 합의에 이르지 못하자, 노동 전문가에게 근로자들과 경영진 사이의 분쟁을 **중재하도록** 요청했다.

이종현T의 Logical Point

합의에 이르지 못한 결과에 대한 내용이므로 정답은 (D)가 된다.

예 시 문 제

1. 정답 : (E)

해석 : 일반적으로 사람들은 화를 내는 것이 틀림없이 심장에 해로울 것이라 생각한다. 2000년에 노스캐롤라이나대학교에서 실시한 한 연구에서 13,000명의 환자들은 자신들이 화를 내는 경향을 평가하는 설문지를 작성했고, 몇 년 후에 추가 조사를 받았다. 그들의 혈압은 분명 정상이었지만, 자주 화를 낸다고 말했던 사람들은 흡연, 당뇨병, 체중 등의 요인을 참작하더라도 나머지 사람들 보다 그 몇 년 동안에 심장마비에 걸릴 확률이 3배 더 높았다. **이와 마찬가지로**, 이스트 런던대학교의 마크 맥더모트(Mark Mcdermott)는 화를 표출하는 사람들이 소리 지르는 것을 참는 사람들보다 심장병에 더 많이 걸린다는 사실을 밝혔다.

이종현T의 Logical Point

이 문제 풀이의 핵심은 연결사 앞의 내용과 뒤의 내용에서 소재가 달라진다는 것이다. 연결사 앞의 문장은 노스캐롤라이나 대학교 실험의 얘기이고 뒷 내용은 런던대학교의 얘기이다. 따라서 소재가 달라졌다. 그런데 하고 싶은 이야기는 심장에 관한 이야기로 같은 얘기이므로 정답은 (E)가 된다.

2. 정답 : (B)

해석 : 여행은 생각의 산파이다. 움직이는 비행기, 배, 그리고 기차가 내부의 대화에 가장 좋다.

이종현T의 Logical Point

뒷 문장에서 moving planes를 journey로 본다면 internal conversation에 해당하는게 빈칸에 들어가면 되므로 정답은 (B)가 된다.

3. 정답 : (A)

해석 : TV 메시지를 처리하는 것은 눈이 프린트된 페이지들을 읽는 것에 대해 직선적으로 처리하는 것이라기 보다는 귀의 한번에 처리하는 과정과 같다. McLuhan에 다르면, 텔레비전은 근본적으로 듣는 매체이다.

이종현T의 Logical Point

TV 메시지들은 귀를 가지고 하는 과정이라고 했으므로 뒷 문장 빈칸에도 귀와 관련된 요소가 들어가면 된다. 따라서 정답은 (A)가 된다.

예 시 문 제

1. 정답 : (D)

해석 : 과학적 엄격함을 수학적인 접근법과 **동일시함으로써**, 사회과학 분야의 연구자들은 종종 수학적인 방법에 잘 맞춰진 그들의 좁게 제한된 주제들에 그들의 범위를 **제한해왔을지도** 모른다.

이종현T의 Logical Point

뒷 문장을 보면 that are 부분에서 수학적인 방법에 잘 맞춘다는 내용이 나와 있다. 따라서 과학적인 것과 수학적인 것을 맞춘다는 내용이 되므로 첫번째 빈칸에는 같게 만들어주는 identifying이나 equating이 들어가면 좋다. 그리고 그 다음 to those narrowly ~부분을 보면 주제의 분야가 좁아지는 것이므로 두번째 빈칸에는 제한하는 의미인 limited가 와서 정답은 (D)가 된다.

2. 정답 : (A)

해석 : 일상의 고된 일 속에서는 권태와 자기연민에 빠져 방황하기가 쉽다. 그러나 어떤 사람들은 삶의 불행을 아주 유연하게 극복할 수 있는 것처럼 보인다. 심지어 가장 우울한 날에도 매리 포핀스(Mary Poppins)의 쾌활함을 뿜어낸다. 이들은 어떻게 그렇게 해내는 것일까? 어떤 사람들은 밝은 성격으로 축복을 받았을지도 모르지만, 누구든 **우울증을 이기도록** 도와줄 수 있는 몇 가지 검증된 방법들이 있다. 종종 그 방법을 실행하는 데는 몇 분밖에 안 걸리지만, 일반적인 삶의 만족과 안녕에 영속적으로 이로움을 줄 수 있다.

이종현T의 Logical Point

이 글은 전체적으로 지루하고 우울한 것들을 이겨내는 것에 대한 얘기다. 그리도 마지막 문장에서 이 기술들은 너의 삶의 만족도와 복지를 높여주는 기술들 이라고 했으므로 우울한 것을 이겨준다는 내용의 정답은 (A)가 된다.

3. 정답 : (A)

해석 : 현대 건축에 관한 과제들과 현대 건축이 해결해야 하는 여러 문제들이 순전히 옛 건물에 새로운 점들을 추가하는 것과 연관된 것은 아니다. 가장 중요한 문제들 중 하나는 현대화라는 문제이고, 이러한 현대화 작업은 당연히 현대 건축의 사용을 의미한다. 문제는 옛 건물의 존속을 보장하기 위해 옛 건물을 보존할만한 가치 있는 것이 되게 하는 그 우수한 점들을 **없애지 않고** 옛 건물의 내부 구조를 변경시켜야 할 경우에 현대 건축적 장치들을 어느 정도로까지 이용하는 것이 필요하고 또 허용되는가 하는 것이다.

이종현T의 Logical Point

뒷 내용을 보면 옛 건물의 내부 구조를 변경한다는 내용이 있으므로 옛 건물의 내용이 바뀐다는 내용이 들어가야 한다. 따라서 정답은 (A)가 된다.

4. 정답 : (B)

해석 : 가장 기본적인 차원에서, 언어는 더불어 살고 있는 무리의 사람들이 의미를 만들어내기 위해 사용하기로 서로 합의한 하나의 공유된 상징 또는 기호의 집합체이다. 선택된 기호와 합의된 의미 사이의 관계는 대단히 **자의적이다**. 우리가 (자의적이라는) 이 개념을 쉽게 예시해보일 수 있는 방법은 친숙한 집안의 애완동물을 나타내기 위해 서로 다른 문화에서 사용하고 있는 다양한 상징(단어)을 살펴보는 것이다. 핀란드에서는 *kissa*라고 정했지만 독일에서는 *katze*가 선택된 반면, 스와힐리 사람들은 *paka*를 사용한다. 보다시피, 이러한 단어들 중에 그 어떤 것도 고양이의 실제 특성과는 아무런 관련이 없다.

이종현T의 Logical Point

마지막 문장을 보면 이런 단어들 어떤 것도 고양이의 실제 특성과는 관련이 없다고 했으므로 단어와 그 대상의 실제 의미와는 관계 없다는 내용이 빈칸에 들어가면 된다. 따라서 정답은 (B)가 된다.

5. 정답 : (D)

해석 : 19세기 자본주의 옹호자들은 자유경쟁시장과 다윈이 설명한 생존경쟁 - 여기서는 적자(適者)가 생존한다. - **사이의 유사성을 이끌어냄으로써** 부유층에 의한 빈곤층 착취를 합리화 했다.

이종현T의 Logical Point

Darwin의 개념을 이용하여 합리화시켰다고 했다고 볼 수 있으므로 옹호자들이 좋아하는 예시라는 것을 알 수 있다. 따라서 둘의 관계가 유사하다고 하는 (D)가 정답이 된다.

6. 정답 : (C)

해석 : 인상파 화가들은 종교 역사 혹은 신화에 관한 전통적인 주제를 따르기보다 우리가 알고 있는 세계의 일상적인 장면들을 그렸다. 그들은 실물 풍경을 보이는 그대로 그렸으며, 비현실적인 과장을 하지 않았다. 그들은 **꼼꼼한** 마무리에는 관심이 없었고, 신속하고 자연스런 붓질로 물감을 칠했다. **쏜살같이 지나가는** 순간순간과 물체가 빛을 반사하거나 흡수하는 방식을 포착하고 자, 모네, 르누아르, 마네, 피사로 등은 캔버스 위에 새롭고 눈부시도록 생동감 넘치는 세상을 그려냈다. 그들은 또한 동료 화가들의 작품에도 영향을 미쳤는데, 이들 가운데는 세잔느, 드가, 반 고흐 등이 가장 유명하다.

이종현T의 Logical Point

첫번째 빈칸에는 신속하고 자연스러운의 반대가 필요하다. 그렇다면 꼼꼼한이 들어갔을 때 조금 느리지만 아주 자세하다는 의미가 가능하다. 그리고 두번째 빈칸에는 신속하다는 것과 같은 맥락의 얘기가 필요하므로 정답은 (C)가 된다.

7. 정답 : (D)

해석 : 시계의 권위에 굴복하도록 강요함으로써, 체계적인 시간기록은 일종의 <u>**독재**</u>를 시행했다.

이종현T의 Logical Point

By forcing ~ clock 까지의 부준과 systematic ~ 부분의 주절이 같은 얘기라고 보면, 앞에서 시계의 권위에 굴복한다고 했으므로, 시계의 개념에 복종하게 된다는 얘기가 주절에도 들어가면 된다. 따라서 시계가 우리를 통제한다는 의미의 (D)가 정답이 된다.

8. 정답 : (B)

해석 : 경찰들은 아이들을 경찰차에 태워서 데리고 다녔고, 무전기를 통해 서로 이야기를 나누게 해줬으며, 아이들에게 아이스크림을 나눠주면서 그날을 <u>**마무리했다**</u>.

이종현T의 Logical Point

시간의 흐름으로 나오므로 끝맺는다는 내용이 필요하다. 따라서 정답은 (B)가 된다.

UNIT 5 예 시

예 시 문 제

1. **정답 : (A)**

해석 : 수많은 역사적인 사료들은 과학자들의 **편견**이 자료의 해석과 그들의 지적 객관성의 **손상**에 주는 가장 중요한 영향을 설명한다.

이종현T의 Logical Point

자료를 해석하는 것과 지적인 객관성이 대조될 수 있는 포인트라는 것을 보는 것이중요하다. 해석은 주관적인 걸로 객관성은 객관적인걸로 볼 수 있기 때문이다. 따라서 편견이 지적인 객관성을 약화시킬 수 있다는 의미의 (A)가 오는 것이 적당하다.

2. **정답 : (B)**

해석 : 보인 계곡(Boyne Valley)에 있는 아일랜드의 석기시대 무덤에서 발견된 개 뼈는 애완견의 **가능한 이중적 기원**을 새롭게 조명하는데 도움을 주었다. 약 5,000년 전의 것으로 여겨지는 개 뼈는 아일랜드 미스(Meath) 주에 있는 뉴그레인지(Newgrange)에서 발굴되었는데, 뉴그레인지는 석기시대의 농부들이 지은 고대 기념물이다. 더블린 트리니티 대학의 과학자들은 그 뼈를 사용해서 그 개의 유전자 배열 순서를 밝혔다. 그 연구는 현대의 개들이 유라시아 대륙의 정반대편 끝에서 늑대에 대한 개별적인 두 개의 가축화 과정을 통해 생겨났을지도 모른다는 것을 암시한다. 그것은 인간의 가장 친한 친구인 개가 아시아에 서식하는 늑대의 단일 사육을 통해 유래되었다는 예전의 이론들과 배치된다.

이종현T의 Logical Point

지문의 중후반 즈음에 that modern dogs부터 wolves까지를 보면 현대의 강아지들이 두 개의 분리된 늑대들의 가축화로부터 나타났다라고 나와 있다. 여기서 두 개의 조상이 있다는 점이 추론 가능하고 정답은 (B)가 된다.

3. **정답 (A)**

해석 : 고대 로마에는 **"말은 날아가 버리지만(사라지지만), 글은 그대로 남는다."** 라는 속담이 있었다. 누군가와 대화를 나누다가든, 영화를 보다가든, 책을 읽다가든, 새롭고, 유용한 단어나 어구를 알게 될 때마다, 당신의 주머니에 있는 핸드폰 또는 노트에 그 정보를 저장하도록 하라. 이러한 방법으로 당신은 시간이 있을 때마다 당신이 기록한 정보를 복습할 수 있다.

이종현T의 Logical Point

뒤의 문장을 보면 노트에 정보를 적어두어야 복습할 수 있다는 것이므로 핵심은 글을 써서 정보를 남겨야 한다는 느낌의 선지가 와야 한다. 따라서 정답은 (A)가 된다.

4. 정답 : (D)

해석 : 세계가 탈세자들을 **<u>덜 반기고</u>** 있다. 그것은 최근에 금융비밀지수(Financial Secrecy Index)에 나타난 결론이다. 금융비밀지수는 90개가 넘는 나라의 재정 투명성과 정보 공유에 대한 다양한 조치를 검토한 다음 각 나라가 비거주자들에게 제공하는 금융 서비스의 수준에 따라 가중치를 준다. 2013년 이후로 대부분의 나라들의 점수가 하락해왔는데, 그것은 투명성이 보다 커졌다는 것을 가리킨다. 한때 조세 피난처로 악명을 떨친 케이맨제도와 룩셈부르크는(점수가) 가장 개선된 나라인데 조세 운동가들은 한때 룩셈부르크를 유럽에 있는 금융 비밀의 '죽음의 별' 이라고 불렀다.

이종현T의 Logical Point

뒷 내용을 보면 투명성이 커졌다는 내용이 나온다. 따라서 탈세하기가 더 어려워졌다는 것을 추론할 수 있고 정답은 (D)가 된다.

5. 정답 : (C)

해석 : **<u>암은 제각기 다르다</u>**. 심지어 환자 개인의 몸속에 있는 종양들도 시간이 지나면서 변할지도 모른다. 그리고 의사들은 어떤 흑생종의 종양이 또 다른 흑생종보다 폐암 또는 뇌종양과 더 많은 공통점을 갖고 있을 수도 있다는 사실을 알아가고 있다. "우리는 모든 폐암은 같고, 모든 유방암은 같으며, 모든 대장암은 같다는 개념을 바꾸고 있습니다."라고 뉴욕 메모리얼 슬로언 케터링 암센터(MSKCC)에서 분자 종양학을 담당하는 크래비스 센터의 국장인 데이비드 솔릿(David Solit) 박사는 말한다.

이종현T의 Logical Point

중간에 "We are moving ~ 이 부분을 보면 모든 폐암이 똑같고 모든 유방함이 똑같고 모든 대장암들이 똑같다는 것으로부터 벗어난다고 나와 있다. 따라서 핵심은 암은 모두 똑같지 않다는 얘기가 되고 정답은 (C)가 된다.

6. 정답 : (A)

해석 : 해석 : 중국의 완곡어구들 가운데 일부도 지나친 신중함으로부터 비롯되었다. 의사들은 환자의 성생활에 대해 묻기보다는 '침실에서 일(방사)'을 하면서 시간을 많이 보내고 있는지를 물어볼지도 모른다. 온라인 사이트들은 문자 그래도 '흥미로운 사랑 상품'을 판매한다. 그러나 중국인들의 에둘러 말하기는 종종 예의

상 불분명하게 표현하는 것의 한 형태이다. 중국인들은 초대나 (많은 기자들이 생각하듯이) 인터뷰 요청을 거절하는 데 있어서 너무 직접적인 것을 꺼려한다. 따라서 중국인들은 흔히 무언가 사정이 여의치 않다고 대답한다. 이는 몇 주내에 다시 청하라는 것을 뜻하지 않는다. **결코 하고 싶지 않음을 의미하는 것이다**.

이종현T의 Logical Point

이 지문의 핵심은 중국인들은 직설적으로 말하지 않고 돌려말한다는 것이다. 그래서 빈칸에 들어갈 말은 돌려 거절하더라도 정말 안하겠다는 의미가 된다는 내용이 들어가야 한다. 따라서 정답은 (A)가 된다.

7. 정답 : (E)

해석 : 나는 종종 밤에 바닥에 놓여 있는 위험한 물건을 발견하고 삼키는 꿈을 꾼다. 그 물건을 토해내려고 기침을 격렬히 하면서 일어나 앉는다. 아내에게 몸을 돌려 치명적일 수 있는 무언가를 삼켰는데 어떻게 해야 하냐고 말한다. 아내는 투덜거리면서 일어나 "조용히 해야! 지금 자려고 하잖아요." 라고 톡 쏘아붙인다. 나는 깜짝 놀라 잠에서 깨어나 그것은 그저 내가 항상 꾸는 똑같은 **악몽**이라는 것을 깨닫고, 다음날 아침 내가 (잠을) 방해한 것을 아내가 기억하지 않기를 바라며 당황스러워 한다.

이종현T의 Logical Point

내가 꾸는 꿈에 대한 얘기인데 그 꿈은 굉장히 위험하다고 되어 있다. 따라서 안 좋은 꿈인 (E)가 정답이 된다.

8. 정답 : (D)

해석 : 열정과 욕망, 그리고 그것들의 연장과 소모는 실제로 아키맨(Aciman, 유대인작가)이 작가로서 크게 집착하고 있는 것일 수도 있다. 인생이란 격렬한 욕망과 그것을 추구하는 짜릿함 속에서 사는 것이다. (아키멘의) 에세이에서 욕망이란 형체가 없으며, 이것이 많은 면에서 욕망을 더 강렬하게 만든다. 아키맨이 상실에 대해 곰곰이 생각한 점은 그가 그 어떤 것도 되찾으려고 애쓰지 않는다는 것이다. 그는 그것을 원하지도 않는다. 종종 주목하기에 너무나도 분명하지만, 욕망의 **완성(성취)**은 곧 그것의 소멸이다. 아키맨이 말하듯이, "완전한 충만함을 누릴 때에는 무엇을 해야 할지를 알지 못한다. 나는 해변을 갖고 싶다. 즉 문을 열면 해변이 있는 것이 내 인생의 꿈이다. 그러나 해변에 가면 나는 항상 실망을 하게 되는데 재미가 없기 때문이다. 당신은 해변에서 무엇을 하는가? 아무것도 할 것이 없다. 그러나 해변에 가는 것에 대해 생각하는 것은 나에게 즐거움을 준다."

이종현T의 Logical Point

빈칸 뒤를 보면 해변에 가면 실망하고 해변에 갈 생각을 하면 즐거움을 준다고 되어 있으므로 이루고 나면 별거 아니다 라는 얘기라는 것을 알 수 있다. 따라서 정답은 이룬다는 의미가 될 수 있는 (D)가 된다.

9. 정답 : (C)

해석 : 한 설문조사에 따르면, 십대의 약 3분의 1이 하루에 100개 이상의 문자 메세지를 보낸다. 일부에서는 십대들이 이와 같은 의사소통 방식에 중독될 수 있다고 우려하고 있다. 한 십대 청소년의 경우 문자메시지를 보내는 것이 호흡하는 것만큼이나 무의식적으로 이뤄진다. 의사들은 문자메시지를 받는 데서 오는 순간적인 **만족감**이 뇌의 쾌락 중추를 자극한다고 말한다. 신경학 연구에 따르면 문자 메시지를 주고받는 십대들의 뇌 영상은 마약 중독자의 그것과 유사하다.

이종현T의 Logical Point

빈칸이 뇌의 기쁜 영역을 자극하는 것이므로 빈칸에도 기쁜 것과 관련된 단어가 필요하다. 따라서 정답은 (C)가 된다.

10. 정답 : (C)

해석 : 일상적인 대화에서 사용되는 몇몇 단어들은 특정 주제의 맥락 내에서 특수한 의미를 가진다. **예를 들어**, 생물학에서 'producers'라는 단어는 할리우드 영화나 브로드웨이 연극을 지원해주는 사람들을 지칭하는 데 사용되지 않는다. 생물학 교과서의 맥락에서 'producers' 는 환경에서 에너지와 원료를 얻고 스스로 음식을 만드는 유기체, 즉 한 범주와 살아 있는 생명체를 지칭하는 것이다. **마찬가지로**, 생물학의 맥락에서 'consumers'라는 단어는 쇼핑객을 지칭하지 않는다. 그것은 스스로 음식을 만들지 못하기 때문에 다른 생명체의 조직과 노폐물을 먹고 살아가야 하는 생명체들을 가리킨다. 특수한 의미를 가진 일상적인 단어들이 교과서에 등장할 때 그 단어들은 일상적인 대화에서는 거의 등장하지 않는 전문 용어들만큼이나 중요하다.

이종현T의 Logical Point

몇몇 단어가 있고 첫번째 단어 이후로 특정 단어가 나오므로 첫번째 빈칸에는 for example이 된다. 그리고 두번째 빈칸에는 다른 단어가 나오므로 소재가 바뀐다. 하지만 하는 내용은 같은 내용이므로 두번째 빈칸에는 similarly가 들어가서 정답은 (C)가 된다.

11. 정답 : (A)

해석 : 몇몇 다른 형태의 '가리개들'처럼, 부르카는 여성을 이방인들이 섞여있는 공공영역이 아닌 일반적으로 가정과 연관 짓는 것의 일부로서, 많은 상황에서 남성 영역과 여성 영영의 상징적인 구분을 나타냈다. 20년 전에 파키스탄에서 활동했던 인류학자 Hanna Papanek은 부르카를 **휴대용 격리장치**로 묘사했다. 친척이 아닌 남성들로부터 여성들을 분리시키고 보호해야 하는 기본적인 도덕적 요건을 여전히 지키면서도 여성들로 하여금 차단된 생활공간에서 벗어나도록 해줄 수 있기 때문에 많은 사람들은 부르카를 자유롭게 해주는 발명품으로 간주한다고 그녀

는 지적했다. 그와 같은 베일(가리개)은 특정한 공동체에 소속되어 있다는 것과 가족이 공동체 조직에서 가장 중요하고 가정이 여성의 신성함과 연관성을 갖는 그런 도덕적 삶의 방식에 참여하고 있다는 것을 의미한다.

이종현T의 Logical Point

빈칸 뒤를 보면 밖에 나갈 수는 있지만 남성들로부터는 여성을 분리시킨다고 되어 있으므로 움직이면서 분리가 된다는 개념인 (A)가 정답이 된다.

12. 정답 : (B)

해석 : '**적자생존**'의 원칙을 연어만큼 잘 보여주는 종(種)은 거의 없다. 초밥의 주된 재료인 연어는 강에서 태어나며, 다 자라고 나면 바다로 이동하고, 새끼를 낳기 위해 태어난 곳으로 힘들게 되돌아간다. 대부분은 태어난 곳으로 돌아가지 못하는데, 최고의 상태에 있는 연어들만이 자신들의 유전자를 물려줄 수 있다.

이종현T의 Logical Point

마지막 부분에 가장 최고의 상태에 있는 종들만이 그들의 유전자를 전달한다고 되어 있으므로 가장 강한 것들이 살아남는다는 것을 알 수 있다 따라서 정답은 (B)가 된다.

13. 정답 : (B)

해석 : 오늘날 법률은 젊은이들의 근로 조건은 물론 근로 시간까지 규정해 놓고 있다. 그러나 항상 그랬던 것은 아니었다. 예를 들어, 20세기까지만 해도 영국의 가난한 가정들의 아이들은 종종 싸구려 노동력으로 착취되곤 하였다. 이러한 착취는 형태가 다양했다. 아홉 살의 어린아이들이 하루에 14시간에서 16시간까지 일해야 했다. 열악한 작업 환경은 아이들의 건강을 심하게 해쳤다. 비록 많은 부모들이 자신들의 자녀들을 보호와 보살핌으로 감싸려고 노력했지만, 그 가족들은 돈이 필요했고 공장주와 광산주들에게 저항할 수 없었다. 많은 아이들은 **버림받았다고** 느꼈음에 틀림없다. 영국의 작가들은 이러한 아동학대를 비판했다. 가령, 유명한 소설가였던 찰스 디킨스(Charles Dickens)는 아이들의 생명이 **비인도적으로** 낭비되는 모습을 종종 묘사하였다.

이종현T의 Logical Point

빈칸 앞 문장을 보면 부모들이 아이를 지켜줄 수가 없다고 나와 있다. 따라서 아이들은 보호를 못 받는다고 느끼는 내용이 첫번째 빈칸에 와야 하고, 두번째 빈칸엔 학대와 관련되 표현이 나와야 하므로 정답은 (B)가 된다.

UNIT 6 시간 / 조건의 부사절 / 구

예 시 문 제

1. 정답 : (C)

해석 : 사태의 심각성을 고려해볼 때, Terrence의 **조소적인** 재담은 적절하지 않았다. 그는 지금이 비꼴 때나 장소가 아니라는 것을 깨닫니 못하는 것 같았다.

이종현T의 Logical Point

앞문장에서 '빈칸'한 말은 적절하지 않았다라고 되어 있다. 세미콜론으로 되어 있으므로 이어지는 문장은 같은 방향이라고 본다. 그랬을 때 뒷문장에서 비꼴 때가 아니라고 했으므로 앞 문장에서 비꼬는 것은 적절하지 않았다는 내용이 나와야 한다. 따라서 비꼰다는 의미가 될 수 있는 (C) sardonic이 정답이다.

2. 정답 : (A)

해석 : 사람들이 존재하는 단어들과 단어를 형성하는 요소들을 사용하면서 새로운 단어들을 구성할 때, 만약 우리가 그 단어들을 형성하기 위해 그들이 이용하는 요소들이 의미하는 것을 알고 그들이 **이용하는** 단어를 형성하는 규칙이 친숙하다면 우리는 쉽게 그것들을 이해한다.

이종현T의 Logical Point

부사절을 보면 존재하는 단어들을 사용하고 단어 형성의 요소들을 사용한다고 나와 있다. 그래서 핵심은 이런 요소들을 사용하는 것이므로 빈칸에는 그들이 사용하는 규칙이 나와야 한다. 부사절의 people과 주절에서 they가 같은 대상이기 때문이다. 따라서 정답은 (A) employ가 된다.

3. 정답 : (B)

해석 : 전체 농구 시즌을 그의 집에서 단 한번도 떠나는 것 없이 본 후에, 그는 그의 다리 근육이 **위축되기** 시작하는 것을 깨달았다.

이종현T의 Logical Point

집을 떠나지 않았다는 내용으로부터 움직이지 않았다는 것을 알 수 있다. 움직이지 않은 상태라면 다리 근육은 위축되므로 정답은 (B) atrophy가 된다.

4. 정답 : (D)

해석 : 그것들을 수행하려는 정치적인 의지 없이, 그러한 야망있는 계획들은 종종 **허망하다**.

이종현T의 Logical Point

them이 가리키는 것은 such ambitious plans이다. 그래서 그런 계획들을 이행하려는 정치적인 의지 없으면, 의지가 없기 때문에 실행할 수가 없다는 의미가 나와야 하므로 실행할 수 없다는 의미에 가장 가까운 (D) forlorn이 정답이 된다.

5. 정답 : (D)

해석 : 만약 남아있는 쿠바의 우수한 선수들이 모두 동시에 시장에 나온다면, 뉴욕 양키즈와 같은 **재벌** 구단들이 돈을 써서 다시 한번 정상에 오를 수 있을 것이다.

이종현T의 Logical Point

쿠바의 선수들이 모두 시장에 나왔고 구단들이 돈을 쓴다고 했으므로 빈칸에는 돈이 많은 구단의 의미가 들어가면 된다. 따라서 정답은 (D) plutocratic이 된다.

6. 정답 : (B)

해석 : 최근의 감소는 대게 기름 때문이다. 가격 하락이 **입혔던** 큰 혼란을 고려해볼 때, 러시아에서 현저히, Ms. Yellen은 뚜렷하게 **낙관적이다**. 그녀는 이것이 성장에 긍정적일 것이라고 확신했다. 왜냐하면 미국이 순수한 오일 수입국가였기 때문이다. 러시아의 미국과의 거래와 금융적인 연결관계는 미미했다. 그녀는 경험이 물가상승의 영향은 **일시적일** 것이라고 시사한 것에 주목했다.

이종현T의 Logical Point

밑에서 세 번째 문장에 러시아와 미국의 연결관계는 미미하다는 내용이 나온다. 계속 같은 얘기가 반복된다고 봤을 때 물가 상승의 영향은 미미할 것이다. 따라서 세 번째 빈칸에는 transitory가 들어간다. 그리고 영향이 미미하다는 것은 상황이 괜찮다는 것이므로 두번째 빈칸에는 sanguine이 들어가도 좋다. 마지막으로 havoc과 잘 연결되는 wrought를 넣어서 정답은 (B)가 된다.

7. 정답 : (A)

해석 : 개인 생각의 자유는 개인의 행동의 자유보다 더 확실하게 **보호되어져야만** 한다. 비록 또한 바람직할지라도 후자가 다른사람들의 자유와 권리에 의해 부과된 제한에 **영향을 받아야만** 하기 때문이다.

이종현T의 Logical Point

given 뒤를 보면 바람직할지라도 후자, 즉 행동의 자유는 제한에 걸린다는 의미가 나옴을 알 수 있다. 그러므로 생각의 자유가 더 중요하다는 내용이 필요하다. 따라서 정답은 (A)가 된다.

8. 정답 : (C)

해석 : 만약 주 정부의 최근의 예산 문제들이 **이례적이였다면**, 그것들을 미래에 근시안적인 국가 재정 계획의 불가피한 영향을 피하려는 노력에 있어서 **분명하게 하려는** 예시로서 이용하는 것은 유용하지 않을 것이다.

이종현T의 Logical Point

부사절과 주절은 같은 내용이라고 보았을 때 그것들을 이용하는 것이 유용하지 않다는 것을 알 수 있다. 따라서 첫번째 빈칸에는 이용할 수 없는 느낌이 들어가야 한다. 그리고 두번째 빈칸에는 좋은 예시로서 이용할 수 없다는 것이 맞다. 따라서 정답은 (C)가 된다.

9. 정답 : (A)

해석 : 만약 효과적인 새로운 약들이 흔히 관찰되고 **평범한** 부작용이 있다면, 그러한 약들은 심지어 실험실 결과가 주의를 하라고 나타낼 때에도 너무 자주 **안전하다고** 여겨진다.

이종현T의 Logical Point

첫번째 빈칸에는 commonly observed와 같은 속성의 얘기가 나와야 하고 두번째 빈칸에는 even이 있기 때문에 caution의 반대 의미가 나와야 한다. 따라서 정답은 (A)가 된다.

10. 정답 : (B)

해석 : 놀랍게도, 옥수수 작물 위에 떨어진 비가 부족하다는 것을 고려해볼 때, 수확량은 **고무적이었다**. 결과적으로, 나라의 옥수수 비축량들은 **고갈되지 않았다**.

이종현T의 Logical Point

Surprisingly라는 단어가 있으므로 비가 많이 안떨어졌어도 수확량은 많다는 내용이 첫번째 빈칸에 와야 한다. 그리고 그 결과에 대한 내용이므로 비축량은 충분했다는 내용이 두번째 빈칸에 들어가야 한다. 따라서 정답은 (B)가 된다.

11. 정답 : (E)

해석 : 그는 이후에 발생할 가능성이 있는 큰 **혼란**을 고려해볼 때 그러한 작은 이점을 얻기 위해 필요로 되어지는 희생을 하는 것은 **현실적이지 않다고** 느꼈다.

이종현T의 Logical Point

in view of 뒤에 intense 가 있으므로 little advantage와는 대조가 된다는 것을 알 수 있다. 따라서 이점의 반댓말의 개념이 두번째 빈칸에 오고 그랬을 때 희생하는 것은 현실적이지 않다는 (E)가 정답이 된다.

12. 정답 : (D)

해석 : 그가 대단히 **고집스러운** 태도로 중재 현장에 왔다는 점을 고려할 때 조화로운 합의를 향한 어떤 진척도 거의 없었다는 것은 매우 당연했다. 다시 말해 그는 완전히 **구제불능**이었다.

이종현T의 Logical Point

어떤 태도가 있어서 합의가 불가능하다는 내용이므로 합의가 불가능한 태도가 들어간다. 그리고 그와 같은 맥락의 얘기가 두번째 빈칸에도 필요하다. 따라서 정답은 (D)가 된다.

Part II 다른 방향

UNIT 1 비교/대조

예시문제

1. 정답 : (D)

해석 : 우리의 노상범죄에 대한 매우 **차별화된** 어휘는 우리의 기업 범죄에 대한 **제한된** 어휘와 현저하게 대조된다, 바로 기업 범죄의 정도에 대해 대중들이 인식하지 못하는 것과 일치하는 사실이다.

이종현T의 Logical Point

contrast로 이어져서 주어와 with 뒤에는 대조가 된다. 그리고 동격으로 이어진 a fact 뒤를 보면 대중들은 기업 범죄의 정도에 대한 인식이 없다고 나와 있다. 따라서 기업 범죄에 대해서는 잘 알지 못하므로 어휘가 적다는 의미의 limited가 들어가야 한다. 그리고 첫번째 빈칸에는 limited의 반대 의미가 될 수 있는 differentiated가 들어가서 정답은 (D)가 된다.

2. 정답 : (E)

해석 : 생물학자는 그들 연구의 피실험자들을 향한 **객관적인** 태도를 유지해야만 하지만, 사회 과학자들은, 역설적으로 개인적인 관여와 학구적인 **객관성**을 통합시켜야 한다.

이종현T의 Logical Point

biologists와 social scientists를 비교하고 있다. whereas로 연결되어 있으므로 둘 사이는 대조된다고 볼 수 있다. 따라서 첫번째 빈칸은 personal involvement의 반대 의미의 단어가 필요하고 객관적이라는 의미의 disinterested가 올 수 있다. 그리고 또 두번째 빈칸은 paradoxically라는 말 이후의 and로 연결되어 있으므로 관계는 반대가 된다는 것을 알 수 있다 따라서 personal involvement의 반대인 detachment가 들어가서 정답은 (E)가 된다.

3. 정답 : (D)

해석 : 비록 많은 사람들이 건강 문제를 다루기 위해 동종요법을 사용할지라도, 다른 사람들은 대신 전동적인 치료법에 **의존하면서**, 그러한 대안 치료법을 **지지하지 않는다**.

이종현T의 Logical Point

conventional medical treatments와 대조되는 것이 alternative treatments와 homeopathic remedies가 된다. 그래서 , 뒤의 내용과 앞의 내용은 반대의 의미가 와야 한다. 그런데 문장에 not이 있으므로 첫번째 빈칸엔 countenance가 오고 두번째 빈칸에 relying on이 오면 두 빈칸이 반대 의미를 만들어주게 된다. 따라서 정답은 (D)가 된다.

4. 정답 : (D)

해석 : 총기 폭력을 **줄이기** 위해 더 강력한 총기 규제법을 찬성하는 이들은 주로 총기 규제에 반대하는 압력단체들의 주장에 반박함으로써 자신들의 주장을 뒷받침한다. 총기 규제법에 찬성하는 이들로서는 행동에 나서야 할 논거(이유)가 압도적으로 많지만, 총기 소유에 대해 개인적으로 (또는 금전적으로) 매우 몰두해 있는, 자기 생각이 **확고한** 소수 사람들을 설득할 가망성은 전혀 없다.

이종현T의 Logical Point

첫번째 빈칸에서는 총기 폭력을 '빈칸'하려는 강력한 법이 필요하다고 했으므로 강한 법을 통해 폭력을 줄이려 한다는 abate가 적절하다. 그리고 두번째 빈칸에서는 총기 보유에 대해서 개인적으로 또는 금전적으로 몰두한 소수라고 했으므로 그 소수는 생각이 확실하다는 의미의 entrenched가 적절하다. 따라서 정답은 (D)가 된다.

5. 정답 : (C)

해석 : 낭만주의에 기초하고 천부인권사상에서 파생되어 나온 유럽의 법률은 대체로 창작자를 보호하는 것을 추구해왔다. **이와는 반대로**, 미국의 저작권 개념은 문화를 상품으로 더 많이 간주한다. 미국의 헌법은 저작권을 작가들의 창작을 장려하기 위해 제한된 기간 동안 작가에게 주어지는 보상으로 규정한다. **하지만** 최근에 미국은 유럽의 선례를 따라 저작권의 기간을 창작자의 사후 70년까지로 연장했다. 이는 창작자의 권리에 대한 뒤늦은 인식에서라기보다는 변화를 위해 계속 로비를 해 왔던 할리우드나 다른 중요한 권리자들에게 양보해서였다. 1998년에 디즈니와 다른 영화 제작사들은 영화에 대한 저작권을 95년까지 연장하는 법안을 밀어붙였고, 그 법안은 '미키마우스 법'으로 알려지게 되었다.

이종현T의 Logical Point

이 지문에서의 핵심은 유럽과 미국이 대조된다는 것이다. 따라서 첫번째 빈칸에는 however나 on the other hand가 나온다. 그런데 두번째 빈칸 뒤로는 미국이 유럽을 따라간다는 내용이 나오므로 또 대조가 된다. 그래서 둘 다 대조의 연결사인 정답은 (C)가 된다.

6. 정답 : (D)

해석 : 1985년과 1986년에 천식의 유행이 바르셀로나를 강타했다. 그 도시의 과학자들은 처음에는 공기오염, 꽃가루, 곰팡이와 같은 유력한 용의자들에 관심을 두었다. 그러나 천식을 알고 있는 사람들과의 일련의 전화 인터뷰를 통해 훨씬 더 정확한 원인을 알게 되었다. 모든 발병이 항구 가까이에서, 그리고 콩을 배에서 내리고 있을 때 일어났다. 그 원인은 콩에서 일어난 먼지임이 분명했다. 그래서 해결책으로 항구의 곡물 저장실에 여과장치를 설치했다. 천식은 전 세계에서 가장 흔한 만성 질환 중 하나이며, 약 3억 명의 사람들이 걸리는 병이다. 그러나 무엇이 천식을 일으키는지는 확실하지 않으며, 결과적으로, 대부분의 천식환자들은 제대로 치료받지 못한다. 바르셀로나의 이야기 같은 **성공** 이야기는 드물다.

이종현T의 Logical Point

지문의 첫 부분에 보면 바르셀로나의 경우엔 원인을 알아서 해결책을 잘 세웠다고 나와 있다. 따라서 바르셀로나의 이야기의 성공이라는 (D)가 적절하다.

7. 정답 : (E)

해석 : 나이가 많은 근로자들은 급여 체계에서 연공서열에 따른 가중치가 반영되어 관례적으로 더 많은 돈을 벌었다. 그래서 퇴직 후에 그들에게 마지막 급여를 기준으로 연금을 주는 비용이 더 높아져 왔다. 고용주들이 의료 서비스를 제공하는 미국에서 나이 많은 근로자들은 보험에 가입하는 데 더 많은 비용이 든다. 다른 한편, 그런 근로자들은 급료에 더 유연할 수도 있는데, 고용주가 나이 많은 사람들이 선호하는 시간제 근무를 기꺼이 제공할 경우에 특히 그러하다. 그것은 나이 많은 사람들은 **고용하기에 더 매력적이도록** 만들 수 있다.

이종현T의 Logical Point

빈칸 앞문장을 보면 나이 많은 사람들은 급료에 더 유연하고 시간제 근무도 기꺼이 받아들일 수 있다고 나와 있다. 따라서 그들을 고용하고 싶다는 의미인 (E)가 정답이 된다.

8. 정답 : (B)

해석 : 짐바브웨 소재 한 국립공원에서 살고 있던 사랑받던 사자 세실(Cecil)이 사냥꾼들에 의해 멀리 유인된 다음에 죽임을 당하고, 노획물로 보여지기 위해 목이 잘렸다는 사실을 전 세계 사람들이 알게 되었을 때, 사람들은 빠르게 격분했다. 세실을 죽인 미네소타 주의 치과의사인 월터 제임스 팔머(Walter James Palmer)는 온라인 상에서 살해 협박을 받았다. 수사가 두 대륙에서 시작되었다. 그러나 세실의 죽음이 불법 밀렵을 새롭게 집중적으로 조명해 왔지만, 다른 사냥꾼들은 자신들만의 노획물을 추구하고 있으며, **이는 완전히 합법적인 일이다.** 그것은 바로 대형동물 트로피 사냥(상업적 목적이 아닌 사냥물을 전시하기 위한 과시용 사냥)의

또 다른 좀 덜 알려진 측면 때문이다. 이것은 특히 사냥할 권리를 부유한 스포츠맨들에게 판매할 수 있도록 감금시켜 키운 동물을 인가받아 몰래 다가가서 사냥하는 것을 말한다. 이러한 사냥을 'canned hunting(사육된 동물을 광활한 울타리에 가두고 하는 사냥)'이라고 한다.

이종현T의 Logical Point

빈칸의 뒷 내용을 보면 그들을 죽일 권한이 있고 그 권한을 팔 수 있다는 얘기가 나온다. 따라서 사냥이 허용된다는 이야기가 뒤에 나온다는 것을 알 수 있고 정답은 합법이라고 하는 (B)가 정답이 된다.

9. 정답 : (A)

해석 : 협상가로서 **비타협적 태도**에 대한 그의 초기 평판을 착각하게 만들 정도로, 모건은 최근 그의 이전의 비평가들이 그를 칭찬하는 더 **회유하는** 자세를 취해왔다.

이종현T의 Logical Point

belie라는 단어가 핵심이다. belie는 주어와 목적어의 관계가 대조되는 명사가 와야 하는 동사이다. 즉 여기서 belying의 생략된 주어는 Morgan이므로 Morgan과 his earlier reputation은 대조되는 개념이 된다는 의미이다. 즉 belying의 목적어인 his earlier reputation for ~ 이 부분과 assumed a more ~ 이 부분이 대조가 된다는 뜻이고 반대가 된다는 의미이다. 그래서 역접의 관계가 있는 단어를 찾아주면 정답은 (A)가 된다.

10. 정답 : (E)

해석 : 자신들에게 명성을 가져다준 것을 떠나고 있는 몇몇 유형의 유명 인사들의 경우, 다음에 무슨 일을 할까라는 질문은 쉽게 다루어질 수 있다. 은퇴한 운동선수는 스포츠 방송 진행자 또는 투자자가 될 수 있으며, 인기 드라마가 끝나는 탤런트는 영화 대본들을 살펴볼 수 있다. 그러나 작가가 은퇴를 할 경우에는 왠지 다르게 느껴진다. 소설을 쓰는 것은 그만두고 떠날 수 있는 직업이라기보다는 **세상을 특정한 방식으로 바라본다는** 것을 증명하는 것이다. 이제 그만둔다고 선언하는 작가에게는 뭔가 앞뒤가 맞지 않는 점이 있다. 그렇다면 은유로 표현되어 작품에 들어간 그 모든 관찰들은 어디로 간단 말인가?

이종현T의 Logical Point

빈칸 뒷 문장을 보면 그가 떠나더라도 그가 했던 표현들은 다 남아있다고 나와 있다. 따라서 그가 세상을 바라보았던 방식에 관련된 내용이 되고 정답은 (E)가 된다.

11. 정답 : (A)

해석 : 대부분 종들은 그들의 지리적인 분배에 있어서 **단절**을 보여준다. 종종 주어진 종은 큰 지리적인 지경에서 발견된다. 그러나 그 범위의 개별 인구들은 널리 **분리되어져 있다**.

이종현T의 Logical Point

:(colon)이 있으므로 동격이 된다. 그리고 두번째 빈칸부터 보면 앞 문장과 but으로 이어져 있으므로 큰 지역에 있지만 인구는 그것에 걸맞지 않다는 의미가 온다는 것을 알 수 있다. 그리고 그것과 첫번째 문장은 동격이므로 첫번째 빈칸에도 비슷한 내용이 들어간다. 따라서 정답은 (A)가 된다.

12. 정답 : (E)

해석 : 쉽게 연구되는 중립적이고 이온화된 Milky Way의 주요한 디스크를 구성하는 **성분**과는 다르게, 우리의 은하를 둘러싸고 있는 **성분**의 요소들은 연구에 더 맞지 않다는 것이 입증되어져왔다.

이종현T의 Logical Point

앞의 내용과 뒤의 내용은 Unlike 때문에 역접이 된다. 그런데 형용사가 둘 다 나와 있으므로 두 명사는 같은 명사가 들어가면 된다. 즉 동일대상이지만 반대 속성을 가지고 있다는 의미이다. 따라서 정답은 (E)가 된다.

13. 정답 : (A)

해석 : **환심을 사려하기는** 커녕, Pat은 항상 **조용히 따르는** 것을 꺼렸다.

이종현T의 Logical Point

Far from이 있기에 앞, 뒤는 비슷하지만 정도의 차이가 있는 단어가 나온다. 따라서 정답은 (A)가 된다.

14. 정답 : (E)

해석 : 지속적인 이미지 하락을 약화시키기는커녕, 그 **저속한** 조각상은 이것의 **엉망이 된** 주변환경의 상징적인 것 같았다.

이종현T의 Logical Point

Far from 뒤를 보면 안좋아지는 것을 막기는커녕 이라고 되어있다. 따라서 주절에서는 막기는커녕 오히려 더 안 좋아진다는 얘기가 들어가면 된다. 그래서 두 빈칸에는 전부 안 좋은 의미가 들어가야 한다. 이에 따라 정답은 (E)가 된다.

15. 정답 : (D)

해석 : 소비자들은 다양한 이유로 과일, 야채, 육류와 그 밖의 제품들을 현지시장(지역시장)에서 구매할지도 모른다. 그들은 대형 슈퍼마켓 체인 회사의 주주들보다는 현지생산자(지역생산자)에게 도움을 주길 원할 수도 있는데, 이는 수천 마일에 걸친 불필요한 상품 운송으로 **해석될 수 있는 것이 야기하는** 해로운 환경 영향을 감소시킨다고 볼 수 있는 지역의 주요 관심사이다.

이종현T의 Logical Point

harmful environmental impacts라고 했으므로 지역시장이 아닌 곳에서의 구매를 의미함을 알 수 있다. 그리고 unnecessary transportaion ~ 이 부분이 원인이고 그 결과 생기는 해로운 영향이므로 정답은 (D)가 된다.

16. 정답 : (C)

해석 : 다른 예술분야에서처럼 조각품들의 상업적 가능성을 재빨리 인식하고 **이용하는** 사람들이 있었다. 중세시대의 웅장한 대성당들 안에 그 당시 조각가들의 작품들이 있긴 했지만, 그 구조물들(대성당들)을 낳은 것은 바로 석공들과 건축사들의 기술 결합이었다. 어떤 점에서, 디지털 세계에서는 그 반대현상이 사실이었다. 3차원 공간에서 여러 사물들을 만들어내고 조작하는 데 필요한 하드웨어와 소프트웨어의 개발은 상업계가 주도했다.

이종현T의 Logical Point

마지막 부분을 부면 상업계가 개발을 주도했다고 되어 있으므로 정답은 (C)가 된다.

17. 정답 : (A)

해석 : 네트워크란 새로운 접점의 추가를 통해 발달되는 열린 구조물이다. 그것들은 전통적인 형태의 사회관계가 가진 위계질서가 있고 체계적인 속성과 비교해 볼 때 좀 더 격식에 얽매이지 않는 속성을 갖는 경향이 있다. 궁극적으로는 어느 정도의 안정된 사회관계 패턴을 형성하긴 하지만, 네트워크는 수평적이면서 상호적이고 좀 더 개방적이고 융통성이 있다. 좀 더 포스트모던적인 네트워크 이론가들 중 일부는 네트워크란 인식론적 중심부와 주변부가 아니라 여러 이론가들, 이론들, 그리고 다수의 사용자들이 이동하고 만나는 여러 접점들의 **분산되어 있는** 네트워크라고 주장하면서, 네트워크의 존재와 인식론적 쟁점을 융합시켜버리는 명백히 반(反) 현실주의적 주장들을 펼치는 경향이 있다.

이종현T의 Logical Point

3번째 문장에 Networks는 수평적이라고 나와 있다. 따라서 힘이 똑같이 나뉜다는 의미라는 것을 알 수 있고 정답은 (A)가 된다.

18. 정답 : (A)

해석 : 역겨움이란 특유의 얼굴표정으로 나타나고 어디에서나 음식과 관련된 금기사항들에 표현돼 있는 보편적인 인간 감정이다. 모든 감정과 마찬가지로, 역겨움은 인간사에 엄청난 영향을 미치고 있다. 2차 세계대전 중에 태평양 지역의 미국인 조종사들은 매우 안전하다고 배운 두꺼비와 벌레들을 먹느니 차라리 굶주리는 쪽을 택했다. 음식에 대한 혐오감은 다른 전통들이 폐기된 후에도 **오랫동안 지속되는** 끈질긴 민족적 징표이다.

이종현T의 Logical Point

마지막 문장의 분사구문을 보면 오래 지속된다고 나와 있다. 따라서 빈칸에도 오래 지속된다는 의미가 들어가야 한다. 고로 정답은 (A)가 된다.

19. 정답 : (E)

해석 : 처음부터, 한 나라의 소유라고 주장하는 것으로부터 바다가 자유롭다는 개념은 상반되는 개념에 의해 도전받았다. 즉, 그 개념은 국가적인 안전과 이익의 이유로 바다에 **울타리를 치는** 개념이다.

이종현T의 Logical Point

바다는 국가의 영토에 대한 주장으로부터 자유로운 개념과 상반되는 내용이 들어가야 하므로 정답은 (E)가 된다.

20. 정답 : (D)

해석 : Marshal Philippe는 다른 이 세기의 어떤 프랑스 시민과도 다르게, 역설적으로 엄청난 존경과 완전한 **경멸**의 대상이었다.

이종현T의 Logical Point

paradoxically가 있으므로 A and B엔 반대되는 개념이 오게 된다. 따라서 veneration의 반대인 (D)가 정답이 된다.

21. 정답 : (C)

해석 : 고고학의 핵심적인 딜레마들 중 하나는 현재 빈약하고 종종 **애매한** 물리적인 증거들로부터 복잡한 고대 사회의 **복잡한 것**들을 재정립하는 것이다.

이종현T의 Logical Point

첫번째 빈칸에는 complex에 관한 얘기가 들어가야 하고 두번째 빈칸에는 meager과 비슷한 얘기가 들어가야 한다. 따라서 정답은 (C)가 된다.

22. 정답 : (A)

해석 : 영어에서 'tickle'이란 단어의 의미는 프로이트(Freud)가 꿈의 작용에 관해 말했듯이,"서로 상반된 것들을 표현하는 똑같은 표현수단"을 사용하고 있어서, 말하자면 거의 대조적인 것이다. 옥스퍼드 사전은 그 단어의 19가지 정의 중에서도 "**불안정한 균형 상태**에서 쉽게 뒤집히거나 불안정하고 위태롭고 안정감이 없고 그러면서도.... 제대로 균형을 잡고 있는"을 언급하고 있다. 또 다른 정의들은 지나치게 잘 믿어버리는 것에서 성적으로 자제심이 없는 것에 이르는 다양한 경험을 묘사한다. 그 단어는 불안정한 것에 대해, 그래서 성적으로 흥분된 것에 대해 언급하고 있다. 'tickle'하는 것은 무엇보다도 종종 즐거움으로 유혹하는 것이다.

이종현T의 Logical Point

빈칸과 뒷 내용이 동격이므로 불안정하고 위태롭다는 내용이 빈칸에 들어가면 된다. 따라서 정답은 (A)가 된다.

23. 정답 : (B)

해석 : 현대세계의 정교화는 개개인의 지능이나 상상력에 달려 있는 것이 아니며, 그것은 협동으로 이루어지는 일이다. 아무도 − 문자 그대로 그 누구도 − 내가 글을 쓰고 있는 컴퓨터는 말할 것도 없고, 책상 위의 연필을 만드는 법도 알지 못한다. 이런 것들을 구상하고, 캐내고, 베고, 추출하고, 합성하고, 결합하고, 제조하고, 시장에 내놓는 방법에 대한 지식은 수천 명의, 때로는 수백만 명의 머릿속에 나뉘어 들어 있다. 인간의 진보는 일단 시작되고 나면 더 이상 인간의 뇌의 크기에 의해 제한되지 않았다. 지능은 **집단적이면서 누적적인** 것이 되었다.

이종현T의 Logical Point

지문의 핵심 내용은 수천명 수백만명이 모여서 방법을 만들어낸다고 나와 있으므로 정답은 (B)가 된다.

24. 정답 : (C)

해석 : 수천 년 동안 문명의 일부였던 잔인한 관행들이 백여 년 사이에 갑자기 폐지되었다. 마녀사냥, 죄수들에 대한 고문, 이단자들에 대한 박해, 비국교도들에 대한 처형, 그리고 이방인들에 대한 노예화가 − 이 모든 것들이 역겨울 정도로 잔인하게 실행되었는데 − **나무랄 데 없는 것에서 상상할 수 없는 것으로** 재빨리 바뀌었다. 페인(Payne)은 이러한 변화들을 설명하는 것이 얼마나 어려운지에 대해 다음과 같이 언급하고 있다. "폭력의 행사가 포기되는 과정들은 종종 매우 예상 밖이고 심지어는 불가사의합니다. 우리가 거듭 마주치게 되는 폭력적 관행들은 너무나 뿌리 깊고 너무나 자기 강화적 이어서 그런 관행들이 극복되었다는 것이 거의 마법 같이 여겨집니다."

이종현T의 Logical Point

과거와 현재를 비교하는 것이다. 과거에는 잔인한 과정들이 잔인하게 실행되었다면 현재는 그것들을 시행하지 않는다는 것이 핵심이다. 따라서 잘못된 것이 없다는 내용과 상상할 수도 없다는 내용의 (C)가 정답이 된다.

25. 정답 : (C)

해석 : 글로벌 세계에서 우리가 직면하고 있는 위협들은 **상호 연결되어 있다**. 부유층들은 가난한 이들을 공격하는 위협들에 취약하며, 그 반대도 또한 사실이다. 미국이나 유럽에 대한 핵무기 테러 공격은 전 세계에 치명적인 영향을 미칠 것이다. 그러나 효과적인 의료체계가 전혀 없는 빈곤한 나라에서의 새로운 치명적인 전염병의 출현도 전 세계에 치명적인 영향을 미칠 것이다.

이종현T의 Logical Point

테러 공격은 모든 사람에게 영향을 주고 치명적인 전염병도 모든 사람들에게 영향을 주니 위협은 모두가 영향을 받는다는 내용이 빈칸에 들어가야 한다. 따라서 정답은 (C)가 된다.

26. 정답 : (E)

해석 : Schlesinger는 지속적으로 타협들을 **비난하는** 그의 동료들에 의해 **칭찬받지 못한** 회유적인 태도를 보였다.

이종현T의 Logical Point

두 가지가 올 수 있다. 그 태도가 인정받아서 그것을 계속 동료들도 인정해주거나 그 태도를 싫어해서 동료들은 그 태도를 싫어한다는 얘기가 나와야 한다. 그랬을 때 정답은 (E)가 된다.

27. 정답 : (E)

해석 : 얼버무리는 코멘트의 한가운데에서, 이 솔직담백한 진술은 이것이 본질적인 메리트가 무엇이든지 간에, 명백하게 **변칙**으로서 두드러진다.

이종현T의 Logical Point

다 얼버무리는 말들 속에 하나의 솔직한 말이 있다는 얘기가 된다. 그래서 이는 보통때와는 다르다는 (E)가 정답이 된다.

28. 정답 : (B)

해석 : 포도 과일 주스는 많은 흔한 약들과 위험하게 반응을 한다. 겨우 몇 번 홀짝 마시는 것도 **치료할 수 있는** 복용량이 **유독한** 양이 되게 할 수 있다.

이종현T의 Logical Point

첫번째 문장에 포도 주스가 약물과 결합하면 위험하다고 나와 있다. 그리고 두번째 문장에서 a few sips는 과일 주스를 마시는 것이라는 내용이 된다. 따라서 뒤에는 위험하게 상호작용한다는 내용이 되어야 하므로 두번째 빈칸에는 toxic이 들어가야 한다. 그리고 앞에는 적정량 혹은 치료할 수 있는 양이 들어가야 하므로 정답은 (B)가 된다.

29. 정답 : (B)

해석 : 운 좋게도 살아서 노령에 이르는 사람은 누구나 주택, 음식, 그리고 의료혜택의 비용을 지불해야 되는 문제에 직면할 것이다. 우리 사회가 해결하려고 애쓰고 있는 문제는 우리가 이러한 문제를 어떻게 대처해야 하느냐는 것이다. 일반적으로, 보수주의자들은 개개인들이 스스로 책임을 져야 한다고 주장한다. 이러한 관점에서 보면, 사람들은 노동(일)과 퇴직을 대비한 체계적인 저축계획을 통해서 그들이 필요로 하는 여러 자원들을 소유하도록 해야 된다. 진보주의자들은 **자립**이 부유층들에게는 좋은 것이지만 충분한 소득을 벌지 못하는 사람들의 경우에는 그렇지 못하다고 주장하고 있다. 그들의 관점으로는 정부주도의 접근방식이 최선이다. 당신이 이러한 이슈에 관해 얼마나 보수주의적인지 또는 진보주의적인지는 다음과 같이 요약될 수 있다. 당신은 저소득층 사람들에게 **경제적 보장**을 제공하는 데 있어서 고소득층 사람들이 어느 정도로 도와주어야 한다고 생각하는가?

이종현T의 Logical Point

첫 부분에는 스스로 책임을 져야한다는 내용이 나와 있다. 따라서 첫번째 빈칸에는 혼자 자립한다는 내용이 필요하다. 그리고 그 뒤에는 가난한 사람들은 혼자 책임지기는 어렵고 도와줘야한다는 내용이므로 두번째 빈칸에는 경제적으로 도와준다는 내용이 필요하다. 따라서 정답은 (B)가 된다.

30. 정답 : (C)

해석 : 최근에 발견된 **원시시대의** 새의 해골은 이 고대 생명체가 오늘날의 새들의 모습을 **예측할 수 있게 해준다는** 것을 나타냈다. 초기의 새들과 파충류의 조상들과는 다르게, 이것은 머리에 이빨을 가지고 있었다.

이종현T의 Logical Point

최근에 발견된 해골은 최근의 새들의 모습을 하고 있다. 따라서 고대 생명체와 오늘날의 새와 같다는 의미가 두번째 빈칸에 들어가고 ancient와 관련된 의미가 첫번째 빈칸에 들어가면 된다. 따라서 정답은 (C)가 된다.

31. 정답 : (C)

해석 : 마르크스(Marx)는 **'왜'**를 설명한다. 다시 말해서, 그는 사회활동을 용이하게도 하고 제약하기도 하는 사회구조의 필요성을 설명한다. 그러나 그는 **'어떻게'**에 대해서는, 즉 자본 이동의 기법(작용방식)에 대해서는 설명하지 않는다. 푸코(Foucault)는 **'어떻게'**를 설명한다. 즉, 그는 권력의 기법(작용방식)을 설명한다. 그러나 그는 **'왜'**에 대해서는, 즉 규율권력의 동기나 목적에 대해서는 설명하지 않는다. 마르크스의 '피설명항'이 하나의 전체를 모색하는 일단의 결론이라면, 푸코의 설명은 하나의 결론을 모색하는 일단의 전제들이다.

이종현T의 Logical Point

첫번째 빈칸 뒤를 보면 사회 구조의 필요성 에 관련된 개념이 빈칸에 들어가야 하고 뒤에를 보면 규율상의 권력의 목적이나 동기부여같은 개념이 들어간다. 즉 그것이 필요한 이유와 관련이 깊으므로 why가 들어가야 한다. 두번째 빈칸에는 자본 이동의 기법과 비슷한 얘기가 들어가야하고, 뒤에도 권력의 기법이라고 나와있으므로 방법인 how가 들어가서 정답은 (C)가 된다.

32. 정답 : (C)

해석 : 모든 사회계층에서 부모들은 자녀들의 교육에 세심한 주의를 기울인다. 노동자 계층과 가난한 부모들은 중산층 부모들만큼이나 자녀들이 학교에서 좋은 성적을 내는 것을 보길 열렬히 바란다. 그러나 그들은 자식들이 그러한 목표에 도달하도록 도와주는 접근 방식이 다르다. 노동자 계층과 가난한 부모들은 종종 학교와 관련된 문제에서 '잘못된 일'을 저지를까 우려한다. 그들은 중산층 부모들보다 교육자들의 전문적인 경험에 대해 훨씬 더 많은 경의를 표하는 경향이 있다. 따라서 노동자 계층과 가난한 부모들은 전형적으로 교직원들에 대해 **요구사항이 많기 보다는** 오히려 **공손한** 태도를 보인다. 그들은 교육자들에게 충고를 하기보다는 그들로부터 지도를 구한다. 그리고 그들은 학교와 가정 사이의 상호연관성을 증진하기 위해 노력하기 보다는 양자 사이의 분리를 유지하려 애쓴다.

이종현T의 Logical Point

중산층과 가난한 계층의 부모를 비교하고 있다. 가난한 계층 부모들이 선생님을 더 존경한다는 내용이므로 첫번째 빈칸에는 존경하고 공손하다는 의미가 들어가야 하고 rather than 뒤에는 그 반대가 될만한 의미가 들어가야 한다. 따라서 정답은 (C)가 된다.

33. 정답 : (D)

해석 : 비록 그는 특히 인도주의적인 사람으로서 잘 알려진 것은 아니었을지라도, 그의 고통을 겪는 사람들에 대한 책임감의 깊은 인식은 진짜였고, 겉보기의 **무관심한** 외모 때문에 잘못 생각되어졌다.

이종현T의 Logical Point

S + belie + O도 둘의 관계가 반대지만 O + be belied by S가 되어도 O와 S는 관계가 반대이다. 따라서 남을 신경쓰는 것과 반대되는 내용인 (D)가 정답이 된다.

34. 정답 : (C)

해석 : 천성이 **기회주의자**가 아니었지 때문에, 다니엘(Daniel)은 그의 공동체에 만연한 문제들을 더 빠르고 더 편의적으로 해결하기 위해 자신의 이상을 **훼손시키려고** 하지는 않았다.

이종현T의 Logical Point

더 편리하고 빠른 해결책을 위해 이상을 어떻게 하지 않는다는 것과 첫번째 빈칸과 관련이 있으므로 둘은 같은 맥락의 얘기가 들어간다. 그랬을 때 정답은 (C)가 된다.

35. 정답 : (C)

해석 : 모방작품은 종종 단 하나의 원본을 모방하는 게 아니라, 여러 원본이 가진 **일정하지 않은** 가능성들을 모방하는 것일 것이다.

이종현T의 Logical Point

하나의 원본이라는 말에는 단 한 개, 즉 정확하다는 의미도 담겨있다고 볼 수 있다. 따라서 그 반대가 된다면 일정하지 않다는 의미의 (C)가 정답이 된다.

36. 정답 : (A)

해석 : 컴퓨터가 지배하는 세상에서 우리 자신의 서투른 능력을 생각하면 마음이 불안해질 수 있다. 우리가 잘 하는 것으로서 컴퓨터가 더 잘하지 않는 것이 있기는 한가? 기계가 우리를 **쓸모없게** 만들고 있는 것일까? 우리의 하드드라이브가 숨어서 은밀히 우리를 비웃고 있을까? 과학자들에 의하면 인간이 컴퓨터보다 우위를 **유지할 수** 있는 기술이 여전히 몇 가지 있다. 인간은 패턴인식에 보다 더 능하고, 감정적인 연결이 가능하며 보다 더 혁신적이다.

이종현T의 Logical Point

첫번째 빈칸은 빈칸 앞 문장과 같은 맥락이므로 우리는 쓸모없다는 의미가 필요하다. 그리고 두번째 빈칸은 그 질문에 대해서 아니라고 하는 이야기의 시작이므로 쓸모 있다는 얘기가 되어야 하고 컴퓨터보다 좋은 점도 있다는 얘기가 필요하다. 따라서 정답은 (A)가 된다.

37. 정답 : (C)

해석 : 니콜라이 고골(Nikolai Gogol)은 주관적인 경험과 견해를 유지하면서 종종 꿈같은 환상의 세계와 현실이 뒤섞여 있는 이야기를 쓰고 있었다. **객관적이고** 전지적 3인칭 시점과 대조를 이루는 제한적인 시험은 독자로 하여금 **편향된** 시각을 통해 이야기 속의 세상을 보게 했다.

이종현T의 Logical Point

as opposed to 뒤에는 필자와는 대조가 되는 것이므로 객관적이라는 말이 필요하다. 그리고 두번째에도 객관적인 것과는 반대되는 주관적인 개념의 단어가 필요하므로 정답은 (C)가 된다.

38. 정답 : (A)

해석 : 개별 부족들마다 차이가 있긴 하지만 태평양 북서쪽 부족들의 조각에는 확실히 구별되는 모티프가 있다. 부족의 조각은 문화적, 종교적 신념들을 상징하면서 주로 인간과 동물의 형상에 초점을 맞추고 있다. 그러나 더 중요한 점은 그 예술이 대단히 **인상주의적**이라는 점이다. 조각가들은 조각할 대상을 확인하기 위해 특정하게 문화적으로 인정된 특징들을 활용한다. 비버를 묘사하기 위해 예술가는 두 개의 긴 앞니와 뚜렷하게 비늘로 덮인 꼬리를 조각할 것이다. 매를 묘사하기 위해 예술가는 매의 얼굴에 도로 놓을 만큼 길게 구부러져 있는 부리를 조각할 것이다. 이런 양식화된 특징들은 예술가에 의해 조각의 미적 요구에 따라 배치되어 그 예술가가 전달하고자 하는 발상이나 인상을 묘사하게 될 것이다.

이종현T의 Logical Point

마지막 문장에 예술가가 전달하고자 하는 발상이나 인상이 드러난다는 얘기가 있으므로 그와 같은 맥락의 이야기가 빈칸에도 들어가야 한다. 따라서 정답은 (A)가 된다.

39. 정답 : (A)

해석 : 물론, 두려움은 위험, 즉 실질적 위험에 대한 정상적 반응으로 도피, 불안, 주의 등과 같은 조건 반사적인 방식의 반응들을 초래한다. 그러나 어린아이는 실질적 위험들에 대해서는 물론이고 많은 가상의 위험들에 대해서도 강렬한 두려움을 보인다. 어린이에게 **두려움을 불러일으키는 상황**을 구성하는 요인들에 대해 심리학자들 사이에 많은 논쟁이 있어왔다.

이종현T의 Logical Point

아이들이 두려움을 느끼는 상황에 대한 이야기이므로 정답은 (A)가 된다.

40. 정답 : (A)

해석 : 정치경제학 즉 경제학은 일상적인 인생사 속의 인간에 관한 연구이다. 경제학은 개인적, 사회적 활동들에 있어서 행복의 물질적 필수요건들을 성취하고 활용하는 것과 가장 긴밀하게 관련된 부분을 연구한다. 그러므로 경제학은 한편으로는 부(富)에 관한 학문이요, 다른 한편으로 더 중요하게는 인간에 관한 학문이다. 왜냐하면 인간의 특성을 자신의 종교적 이상에 영향을 미치는 요인이 아니라면 다른 어떤 요인들보다, 자신의 일상적 노동과 노동함으로써 얻게 되는 물질적 자원에 의해 형성되었기 때문이다.

이종현T의 Logical Point

첫번째 빈칸 앞부분에서 첫 빈칸 추론이 가능하고 두번째 빈칸은 빈칸 뒤에서 추론 가능하다. 따라서 정답은 앞 부분엔 물질적인 얘기가 나오므로 wealth가 되고 뒷 부분엔 인간의 특성에 대해 나오므로 정답은 (A)가 된다.

UNIT 2 역 접

예 시 문 제

1. **정답 : (E)**

해석 : 대중교통 이용을 증가시키려는 지방자치 정부의 노력에도 불구하고, 많은 사람들은 버스 스케줄이 너무 **불규칙해서** 의존할 수가 없다고 불평하면서 계속해서 그들의 차를 운전했다.

이종현T의 Logical Point

Despite가 나왔으므로 주절과는 정반대의 내용이고 Despite 뒤에 대중교통을 살리려고 노력했다는 내용이 나왔으니 그 뒤의 주절엔 그 노력이 소용 없다는 얘기가 필요하다. 그리고 그 주절에는 대중교통을 이용하지 않고 그들의 차를 이용한다고 되어 있다. 스케줄과 관련된 내용을 찾는 것인데 의존할 수 없는 이유는 스케줄이 불규칙해서 이므로 정답은 (E) erratic이 된다.

2. **정답 : (D)**

해석 : 비록 차 소유주들이 때때로 전체적인 자동차 수리소에 대해선 **업신여길지라도**, 그들은 그들 자신들만의 수리공들을 같은 태도로 대하는 것을 꺼린다.

이종현T의 Logical Point

핵심은 as a whole이라는 것과 their own이 반대되는 표현이라는 것을 발견하는 것이다. 그리고 그들 자신들만의 수리공들은 안좋게 보기를 꺼린다는 내용이 주절이므로 반대인 부사절에선 전체적인 수리공들은 안좋게 본다는 내용이 들어가야 한다. 따라서 정답은 (D) disdainful이 된다.

3. **정답 : (C)**

해석 : 비록 그 조사는 학문의 여러 분야가 관련된 과정으로 지정되었을 지라도, 이것은 진짜 실제의 과목들의 **통합**을 포함하지는 않는다.

이종현T의 Logical Point

부사절에서 그 조사는 학문의 여러 분야가 관련된 과정이라고 했으므로 여러 학문이 서로 연관되었다는 것을 알 수 있다. 그렇지만 실제 과목들의 ____는 아니라고 했으므로 그래도 그정도까지는 아니라는 것을 알 수 있다. 관련은 되어 있지만 완전 통합까지는 아니라는 것을 알 수 있고 정답은 (C)가 된다.

4. 정답 : (C)

해석 : 그 어떤 사업타당성 연구도, 환경영향평가 보고서도, 경영사례도, 재무 계획도 발표된 적이 없다. 대신에, 어떻게 일자리를 대량으로 창출하고 가난을 끝낼 것 인지에 관해 다니엘 오르테가(Daniel ortega)가 이끄는 샌디니스타(Sandinista) 정부로부터 **진부한 말**만 나오고 있다.

이종현T의 Logical Point

첫번째 문장에 사업타당성 연구, 환경영향평가 보고서 등등이 없다고 나온다. 이는 이것들이 필요한데 아직 없다는 내용이 된다. 그리고 Instead가 나왔으므로 뒷 내용은 필요한 것들은 없고 필요 없는 것들만 있다는 내용이 오면 된다. 따라서 정답엔 진부한 말 이라는 (C) platitudes가 오면 된다.

5. 정답 : (B)

해석 : 로스앤젤레스에 있는 5대 환류대 연구소(Five Gyres Institute)의 마커스 에릭슨(Marcus Eriksen)은 다국적 팀 동료들과 함께 바다에 있는 플라스틱의 양을 추정하기 위해 부유물에 대한 해양지리학적 모델을 만드는 연구를 했다. 이번 주에 『플로스원(PLOS ONE)』에 발표된 연구결과에 따르면, 전체 26만 8,940톤의 플라스틱 가운데 75퍼센트 이상을 200밀리미터 이상의 크기를 가진 물체들이 차지하고 있다. 해양 부유 물체의 수에 관해서, 연구원들은 모두 크기의 플라스틱 조각이 5조 2,500억 개에 달할 것으로 계산했다. 대부분에 해당하는 약 4조 8,000억 개는 미세 플라스틱이고 전 세계에 걸쳐 퍼져있었다. **비록** 미세 플라스틱의 수가 매우 커 보**일지라도**, 이는 연구원들이 생각하는 것보다 훨씬 더 적은 수치였다. 틀림없이 가장 작은 크기의 미세 플라스틱이 큰 조각들에 비해 더 많을 것인데, 이는 작은 조각들이 태양광선과 다른 풍화작용의 영향에 의해 끊임없이 더 작은 조각들로 분해되고 있기 때문이다. **실제로는 정반대가 사실이었는데**, 이것은 다른 어떤 메커니즘들이 해양 표면으로부터 가장 작은 입자들을 없애고 있다는 것을 암시한다.

이종현T의 Logical Point

A는 부사절과 주절에서 huge와 대조되는 lower가 있으므로 역접이 되는 Although나 Even though가 적절하다. 그리고 B에서는 tiny ones가 degraded into fragments가 되면 더 잘게 쪼개져서 더 많아진다는 의미이다. 그런데 B 뒤에는 제거한다는 의미가 나오므로 둘은 또 대조가 된다. 따라서 정답은 (B)가 된다.

6. **정답 : (D)**

해석 : **비정상적인 애착임에도 불구하고, 이러한 수작업 인쇄로의 회귀 현상은 실제로 존재하며 또한 널리 퍼져있다.** 지난 몇 년간, 새로운 세대의 예술가, 그래픽 디자이너, 그리고 디지털 생활에 익숙해져 있는 사람들은 500여 년 전에 요하네스 구텐베르크(Johannes Gutenberg)가 발명한 이래로 거의 변하지 않은 공정을 재발견했다. 데이비드 주리(David Jury)는 『수제품의 매력』이라는 부제가 붙은 그의 저서에서 활자 인쇄는 '너무 오래되어 새롭기까지 하다'라고 말했다. 온라인 명함 제작업체인 MOO는 심지어 8개의 활자 인쇄 도안을 내놓기까지 했다.

이종현T의 Logical Point

문장으로 나온 경우는 주제를 잡아야 하는 문제이다. 이 글의 주제는 수작업 인쇄가 다시 인기가 있어지고 있다는 것이다. 그렇게 봤을 때 정답이 될 만한 것은 (C)나 (D)가 되는데 (C)의 내용이 나오려면 실제로 레이저 프린터기 판매에 대한 내용이 있어야 하는데 지문에는 없으므로 정답은 (D)가 된다.

7. **정답 : (B)**

해석 : 1991년 걸프 전쟁에서 이라크 군대는 전투 계획서를 만들기 위해 미국산 컬러복사기를 사용했다. **그것은 실수였다.** 일부 복사기에 들어 있던 회로에는 은폐된 송신기들이 들어있었는데 이것이 이라크군의 위치를 미국의 전자전(電子戰) 항공기에 노출시켜 폭탄 공격에 미사일 공격의 정확도를 높여주었다. 그 작전은 첨단 전자전에서의 비밀 전선(戰線)을 부각시켜주는데, 이 전선은 적의 자산(강점)을 부채(약점)로 변화시키는 것이다.

이종현T의 Logical Point

빈칸 앞문장은 이라크군이 컬러 복사기를 사용했다는 것이고, 뒷 문장에서는 그걸 통해 미군이 더 미사일 공격을 정확하게 했다는 내용이 나와 있다. 따라서 이라크에게는 안좋은 결과이므로 정답은 (B)가 된다.

8. **정답 : (B)**

해석 : 높은 소프트웨어의 가격은 널리 퍼진 불법 복사**로부터 발생된다고** 빈번하게 말해진다, 비록 높은 가격이 복사의 원인이라고 하는 정 반대가 동등하게 이치에 맞을지라도.

이종현T의 Logical Point

부사절을 보면 정반대의 얘기가 나와 있고 그 동격은 높은 가격이 불법 복사의 원인이라고 나와 있다. 따라서 앞 문장에서는 불법 복제 때문에 가격이 높아졌다는 반대 얘기가 필요하다. 즉 불법 복사가 원인이고 높은 가격이 결과가 되어야 하므로 정답은 (B)가 된다.

9. 정답 : (B)

해석 : Arruthers의 최근의 문학 비판은 그녀의 정곡을 찌르는 코멘트에 대한 평판을 **잘못되었다고 생각하게 한다**. 아주 흥미로운 제목과 책 커버에 대한 지나친 칭찬에도 불구하고 이것은 겨우 **진부한 말**들의 모음정도이다.

이종현T의 Logical Point

Despite의 부사구와 뒤의 주절은 역접의 관계이다. 즉 매우 흥미로운 제목이라고 되어 있으므로 주절에는 흥미롭지 않다는 얘기가 들어가야 한다. 그리고 그 흥미롭지 않다는 것이 첫번째 문장의 최근의 비판이므로 첫번째 문장의 주어와 목적어와는 반대가 된다. 따라서 정답은 (B)가 들어가면 가장 좋다.

10. 정답 : (C)

해석 : 이것이 거의 보편적으로 **금지되어진다는** 사실에도 불구하고 계약 하인의 관행은 여전히 세계의 많은 부분에서 **지속된다**.

이종현T의 Logical Point

Despite로 연결되어 있으므로 빈칸은 서로 반의어관계이다. 보편적으로 금지가 되었지만 여전히 있었다는 정답은 (C)가 된다.

11. 정답 : (C)

해석 : Phaistos의 Minoan 지역에서 발견되는 특별한 점토 디스크는 종종 이것의 권리를 이 수준까지는 지켰던 학자들에 의해 프린팅의 가장 초기의 예시로서 **제시된다**. 다른 프린팅 인공물에 대해서 제시되어진 동등한 주장에도 불구하고.

이종현T의 Logical Point

제시되어진 다른 주장에도 불구하고 이 주장이 없어지지 않았다는 것이므로 정답은 (C)가 된다.

12. 정답 : (C)

해석 : 많은 비평가들에도 불구하고 읽는 것을 가르치는 전체 언어의 철학은 교육자들 사이에서 지속적으로 **신임**을 얻고 있다.

이종현T의 Logical Point

첫번째 빈칸과 두번째 빈칸은 반대 관계가 된다. 반대가 될 수 있는 선지는 (C)가 된다.

13. 정답 : (D)

해석 : 비록 그의 계획에 대해서는 **말이 없었을 지라도**, 그 남자는 그의 관계자들에게 어떠한 사생활도 허용하지 않았고 그들이 다음에 무엇을 할 의도인지에 대해서도 지속적으로 정보를 **간청했다**.

이종현T의 Logical Point

부사구와 주절은 반대 관계이다. 그래서 말이 없는 것과 간청하는 것이 연결되어 정답은 (D)가 된다.

14. 정답 : (C)

해석 : 아무리 그들이 **독창적이었을**지라도, 로마의 시인들은 그들이 **모방한** 몇몇 가장 좋아하는 초기의 작가들을 가지고 있어야 했다.

이종현T의 Logical Point

However s v의 형태가 나와도 주절과는 반대가 된다. 그래서 빈칸에는 서로 반대되는 느낌의 단어가 들어간다. 그랬을 때 정답은 (C)가 된다.

15. 정답 : (C)

해석 : 비록 아일랜드의 문학이 16세기 이후 지속적으로 번영해왔을지라도, **비교할만한** 전통은 시각 예술에서는 **없다**. 우리는 아일랜드의 문화를 단어의 관점에서 생각한다, 시각적 이미지의 관점이 아니라.

이종현T의 Logical Point

마지막 문장을 보면 아일랜드의 문화를 단어의 관점에서 보고 시각 이미지의 관점에서는 안본다고 나와 있다. 따라서 단어가 문학이고 이미지를 visual art라고 보면 둘은 대조가 된다는 것을 알 수 있다. 따라서 그만한 것은 시각예술에서는 없다고 되는 (C)가 정답이 된다.

16. 정답 : (E)

해석 : 비록 단어의 의미는 필연적으로 변할 것 같을지라도, 반드시 사전 편찬자가 스펠링을 수정할 수 없다는 것은 아니다. 대단히, **지속적으로**.

이종현T의 Logical Point

단어의 의미가 필연적으로 바뀐다고 해서 사전 편찬자가 바꿀 수 없다는 것이 아니라 바꿀 수 있다는 의미가 되어야 한다. 따라서 지속적으로 바꿀 수 있다는 의미를 만들어줄 수 있는 (E)가 정답이 된다.

17. 정답 : (B)

해석 : 대부분의 동물 정신과 의사는 동물들이 고의로 야생에서 자살을 시도하는 증거는 없다고 주장한다. 연구자들은 현재 한꺼번에 대량으로 죽는 레밍은 동시에 함께 이주하는 개체들의 밀집한 인구의 불행한 결과이다. 애완동물들이 주인을 따라 죽는 경우에는, 이것은 사회적 유대관계의 혼란으로 설명 될 수 있다. 동물은 죽겠다고 하는 **의식적인 결정을 하지 않는다**. 대신에, 동물들은 너무나도 그의 주인에게 익숙해져서 이것은 더 이상 다른 사람으로부터 음식을 받아들일 수가

없다. 이것이 배우자가 죽은 후의 사람처럼 자살했다고 생각하는 것은 단순히 로맨틱한 인간 해석 스타일의 반영이다.

이종현T의 Logical Point

뒷 문장을 보면 동물들이 자살하는 것 같은 모습은 인간들의 해석이 만들어낸 거지 실제로는 그런 것이 아니라고 나와있다. 따라서 정답에는 자기가 결정한다는 의미인 (B)가 들어가면 된다.

18. 정답 : (E)

해석 : 기업들은 직원들을 해외로 파견하는 것에 많은 생각을 할애하고 있다. 기업들은 가장 전도유망한 직원들에게 해외 근무를 제공한다. 기업들은 더 높은 연봉과 많은 수당을 통해 (대상자의) 환심을 사려고 하며, 때로는 배우자들의 구직을 도와주기도 한다. 그러나 **그 직원들을 본국으로 데려오는** 경우에는, 이야기가 달라진다. 한 연구에 의하면, 1/4에 달하는 회사가 본국으로 돌아오는 직원들에게 전혀 도움을 주지 않는다고 한다. 많은 다른 회사들은 기껏해야 몇 개의 웹사이트 링크를 제공한다.

이종현T의 Logical Point

But 앞 내용은 직원들을 아주 극진하게 대한다는 내용이고 But 뒤에는 직원들을 제대로 대우해주지 않는다는 얘기가 나온다. 따라서 앞의 상황과 반대 상황임을 알 수 있다. 앞의 상황이 직원들을 외국으로 보낼 때이므로 반대 상황이라면 다시 돌아올 때라고 추론할 수 있다. 따라서 정답은 (E)가 된다.

19. 정답 : (B)

해석 : 비록 빽빽하게 인구가 밀집된 지역들에서 심각한 자동차하고의 위험성이 더 높은 것이 **자명한** 것 같을지라도, 그러한 사고는 드문드문 밀집한 지역에서 발생할 가능성이 더 높다.

이종현T의 Logical Point

부사절과 주절은 반대가 된다. 빽빽한 지역에서 사고가 많은 것이 당연한 것 같지만 오히려 인구가 없는 지역에 사고가 많다는 내용이 필요하므로 부사절엔 당연하다는 의미가 될 수 있는 (B)가 정답이 된다.

20. 정답 : (E)

해석 : 비록 몇몇 대표들은 상대측의 제안에 **독설에 찬** 반응을 돌려줬을지라도, 대부분은 상대방의 진술을 **정중하게** 받아들였다.

이종현T의 Logical Point

부사절과 주절은 마찬가지로 역접이 된다. 두 단어가 반대가 되는 것을 찾는 것이다 그랬을 때 정답은 (E)가 된다.

21. 정답 : (A)

해석 : 비록 보통 **소심할지라도**, Alison은 그 문제에 대해서 너무나도 강하게 느껴서 그녀는 그의 말 없음을 잠시 미뤄두고 위원회 회의에서 발언했다.

이종현T의 Logical Point

그녀가 말이 없는 성격을 따로 떼어두고 말을 했다는 내용이므로 부사절에는 말이 없다는 내용이 들어가야 반대가 된다. 따라서 정답은 (A)가 된다.

22. 정답 : (D)

해석 : 우리가 다른 사람들에 반대해서 제기한 비난은 우리 스스로에 대한 **경고**가 되어야만 한다. 그들은 도덕적 행동 코드와 관련한 우리 부분에 대해 쉽게 판단하고 자기만족을 **정당화하려고** 해서는 안 된다.

이종현T의 Logical Point

다른 사람들을 비난한다고 해서 우리 스스로는 용서해주면 안 된다는 것이다. 다른 사람들을 비난하면서 우리는 자기만족 해서도 안 된다는 이야기이다. 따라서 정답은 (D)가 된다.

23. 정답 : (B)

해석 : Michael에 대한 속임수는 그의 아들을 위해 착각의 질서정연함을 **보여주는** 것이었다. 오로지 밤에만, 그의 아들이 잠을 잘 때, 마이클은 그가 그의 아들로부터 숨겨온 혼란을 **인정할 수 있었다**.

이종현T의 Logical Point

첫 문장의 착각의 질서정연함은 실제로는 그렇지 않은데 질서정연한 것처럼 보이게 만든다는 뜻이다. 그리고 그 뒤에 숨겨져 있는 것은 뒷 문장의 chaos이다. 따라서 마이클은 아들에게 혼란을 숨기고 있는 것이다. 그래서 첫 빈칸에는 착각을 진짜처럼 보여준다는 의미가 들어가고 두번째 빈칸은 혼란을 드러낸다는 얘기가 나오면 된다. 고로 정답은 (B)가 된다.

24. 정답 : (E)

해석 : 그는 그의 폭로에 대해서 감사함을 기대했다. 그러나 대신에 그는 적대감에 가까운 **무관심**을 마주했다.

이종현T의 Logical Point

빈칸에는 gratitude의 반대말이 될 만한 단어가 들어가야 한다. 따라서 정답은 (E)가 된다.

25. 정답 : (B)

해석 : 2003년 이후로 조류독감으로 인해 330명이 넘는 사람들이 목숨을 잃었다. 이는 많다고 들리지 않을 수도 있지만, 지금까지 알려진 발병 환자 570명 중 60퍼센트에 해당된다. 사망자 수가 더 높지 않은 단 하나의 이유는 환자들이 조류로부터 직접 바이러스에 감염되었기 때문이다. 다른 모든 사람들에게는 다행스럽게도, 이 바이러스는 사람에서 사람으로 쉽게 옮겨지지 않는다. **그렇지만 옮겨질 수도 있다.** 그것이 지난해 두 팀의 과학자들이 행한 연구의 요지이다. 그들은 조류독감 바이러스의 유전자에 수정을 가하여 공기를 통해 흰 족제비들 사이에 전파될 수 있는 변종을 만들었다. 그리고 흰 족제비는 인간에 대한 적절한 대리물이다.

이종현T의 Logical Point

빈칸 앞에는 바이러스가 옮겨지지 않는다는 내용이고 빈칸 뒷 내용은 바이러스가 옮겨지는 실험에 관한 내용이므로 반대가 된다. 따라서 정답은 (B)가 된다.

26. 정답 : (C)

해석 : **즉흥적임**은 그 자체로 훌륭한 것이지만, 계획, 조직, 세심하고 책임감 있는 계산의 필요성과 완전히 조화될 수 있는 것은 아니다. 가장 고상한 목표인 진실에 대한 추구는 인간이 바라는 행복과 완전히 조화될 수 있는 것은 아닌데, 이는 비록 내가 진실의 추구라는 불치병을 앓고 있다는 것을 알고 있다고 할지라도 이것이 나를 더 행복하게 또는 더 자유롭게 해주지는 않을 것이기 때문이다. 나는 항상 평화와 흥분, 또는 지식과 행복한 무지 사이에서 선택을 해야 된다.

이종현T의 Logical Point

마지막 문장을 보면 지식과 무지가 대조되어 있다. 따라서 첫번째 문장에서도 planning과 대조되는 것이 와야 한다. 따라서 정답은 (C)가 된다.

27. 정답 : (E)

해석 : 관찰을 위한 별개의 카테고리를 확립하는 것의 필요성은 빈번하게 완벽한 **추론**을 하는 시도를 야기시킨다. 실제로는 겨우 **근사치**들만 있을 때에도.

이종현T의 Logical Point

부사절에 in reality가 있으므로 주절과는 반대가 된다는 것을 추론해볼 수 있다. 따라서 주절에는 absolute라는 단어가 있으니 부사절에는, 즉 두번째 빈칸에는 완전하지 않고 정확하지 않은 의미의 단어가 들어가야 한다. 그래서 정답은 (E)가 된다.

28. 정답 : (A)

해석 : 비록 자신의 선거운동에 대한 후원자들의 상당한 기부 때문에 기업의 이익을 위해야 할 의무감을 분명 느꼈지만, 그 후보자는 그 기업들의 현안에 대한 자신의 성실한 지지가 **거짓이라고 생각하게 해주는** 공약 선언을 했다.

이종현T의 Logical Point

부사절과 주절은 반대가 되므로, 기업의 이익에 따를 의무감을 느꼈지만 그 의무감을 지키지 않았다는 내용이 주절에 와야 한다. 그래서 기업의 이익에 따르지 않는다는 의미를 만들어줄 수 있는 (A)가 정답이 된다.

29. 정답 : (A)

해석 : 인기있는 화가는 종종 불쾌하게 행동한다. 그러나 그의 행동은 다른 사람들에 의해 **용납된다** 왜냐하면 그의 **달인급의** 능력 때문이다.

이종현T의 Logical Point

but으로 역접이 되어있다. 불쾌하게 하지만 인정 받는다는 내용이 필요하다. 따라서 정답은 (A)가 된다.

30. 정답 : (A)

해석 : 나는 네 살이었고, 날씨가 습한 켄터키에서 야외에서 놀고 있었다. 할아버지의 트럭을 보고 "할아버지가 저렇게 볼품없는 트럭을 몰아서는 안 돼."라고 나는 생각했다. 그때 나는 페인트 한 통을 발견했다. 그리고 좋은 생각이 떠올랐다! 나는 붓을 들고 트럭에 온통 흰 물방울무늬를 칠했다. 내가 페인트칠을 마무리 하면서 트럭 위에 있었을 때, 할아버지가 마치 넋이 나간 것 같은 표정으로 다가 왔다. "안젤라(Angela)야, 내가 본 것 중에서 가장 멋진 트럭이로구나!" 가끔씩 나는 어른들이 아이의 시각으로 상황을 보려고 하지 않는다고 생각한다. 할아버지는 나를 크게 혼낼 수도 있었지만, **화를 내는 대신에 어린 나의 마음을 북돋아 주었다.**

이종현T의 Logical Point

앞 문장에 그는 나를 혼낼 수도 있지만 그렇지 않았다는 내용이 나와 있다. 따라서 빈칸에는 혼낸 것과는 반대되는 내용이 들어와야 한다. 그래서 정답은 (A)가 된다.

31. 정답 : (A)

해석 : 경제 발전의 주된 동력은 개개인들의 노력과 창의성이다. 개개인들로 하여금 노력하고 발명하게 만드는 것은 그들 스스로 자신의 운명을 통제하도록 내버려두는 자유로운 분위기이다. 만약 개개인들이 다른 사람들이 그들에 대한 책임을 지고 있다고 생각한다면 개개인들의 노력은 **약해질 것이다**. 만약 다른 사람들이 그들에게 무엇을 생각하고 믿어야 할지에 대해 말한다면, 그 결과는 동기부여와 창의성의 상실이거나 복종 아니면 반발이라는 선택이 될 것이다. 그러나 복종도 반발도 발전을 이끌어내지는 못한다. 복종은 **혁신가**들이 없는 사회를 남기고 반발은 건설적인 노력에 쏟아야 할 에너지를 저항 쪽으로 돌려놓는다.

이종현T의 Logical Point

첫번째 빈칸 뒷 문장을 보면 다른 사람들이 말하는대로 하면 동기부여가 없어진다고 나와 있다. 따라서 첫번째 빈칸에 개인의 노력은 약해지고 없어진다는 내용이 들어가야 한다. 그리고 두번째 빈칸을 보면 복종하는 것은 결국 창의성이 없는 사회인 혁신가가 없는 사회가 된다고 볼 수 있으므로 정답은 (A)가 된다.

32. 정답 : (E)

해석 : Dorothy Parker의 비꼬는(신랄한) 재치는 그녀에게 엄청난 명성을 가져다주었다. 그러나 그녀는 결국 Vanity Fair에서 해고되었다. 왜냐하면 잡지사의 편집자가 그녀의 과도하게 **신랄한** 스타일을 반대했기 때문이다.

이종현T의 Logical Point

첫 문장에서 그녀는 신랄한 스타일로 인기를 얻었다고 되어 있으니 편집자도 그녀의 신랄한 스타일을 반대하는 것이 맞다 따라서 정답은 (E)가 된다.

33. 정답 : (E)

해석 : Georgia O'Keefe의 그림을 그리는 능력은 그녀의 커리어의 끝으로 향하면서 시력의 문제 때문에 **악화되었다**. 그러나 그녀는 **인내했고**, 계속해서 연필과 숯으로 그렸다 그녀가 90살을 넘을 때까지.

이종현T의 Logical Point

시력 문제에 의해 생긴 것이므로 능력은 안좋아졌다는 것을 알 수 있고 but이 있으므로 그래도 포기하지 않았다는 내용이 필요하다. 따라서 정답은 (E)가 된다.

34. 정답 : (A)

해석 : 올림픽은 Theodosius 1세에 의해 393년에 금지되었다. 그러나 유럽인들은 그러한 **금지**에도 불구하고 지속적으로 올림픽을 개최했다.

이종현T의 Logical Point

앞에서 금지를 했지만 계속 개최했다는 내용이므로 in spite of 뒤에는 금지의 얘기가 들어가야 한다. 따라서 정답은 (A)가 된다.

35. 정답 : (D)

해석 : 비록 Kepler은 행성의 움직임을 올바르게 설명했던 시스템을 **개발한** 인물일지라도, 그는 완전한 이로을 **공식화하는데에는** 성공하지 못했다.

이종현T의 Logical Point

부사절과 주절은 반대이다. 시스템을 처음으로 '빈칸'하지만 completely theory까지는 성공하지 못했다는 내용이 오는 것이 맞다. 따라서 발견하긴 했지만 완성시키지는 못했다는 (D)가 정답이 된다.

36. 정답 : (B)

해석 : 읽기는 역사적으로 페이지에서 독자와 단어들간의 배타적인 교환이었다. 그러나 상호작용하는 기술들은 이것을 훨씬 덜 **고립적인** 활동으로 바꿨다.

이종현T의 Logical Point

but으로 역접이 되어 있다. 읽기라는 것은 과거엔 제한이 있는 교환이었지만 서로 상호작용이 가능해지면서 더 서로 제한이 없이 교환할 수 있다는 내용이 오는게 맞다. 따라서 less가 있으므로 정답은 (B)가 된다.

37. 정답 : (B)

해석 : 비록 독재 정권에서 **반체제 인사**들이 민주적인 개혁에 대한 욕망이 진심일지라도, 그들은 즉각적인 변화를 야기시킬 가능성은 없다.

이종현T의 Logical Point

주어에는 민주적인 개혁을 열망하는 사람들이 나와야 하고 독재적인 정권을 싫어하는 사람이 들어와야 한다. 따라서 정답은 (B)가 된다.

38. 정답 : (A)

해석 : 비록 회사 밖의 많은 사람들이 그 회사의 성공을 대표의 선견지명으로 돌렸을지라도, 내부의 사람들은 이 성공이 그 대표가 보여줬던 **예지력** 보다는 그 대표의 단호한 태도였다는 것을 깨달았다.

이종현T의 Logical Point

부사절과 주절은 역접이지만 주절안에서 than은 또다시 역접이다 따라서 than 뒤의 빈칸에는 선견지명과 비슷한 단어가 들어가야 한다. 따라서 정답은 (A)가 된다.

39. 정답 : (C)

해석 : 여성에대한 연구해서 상당한 성장이 있었음에도 불구하고, 여성 노동의 역할은 유럽 산업화의 역사의 경제적인 분석에서 하나의 가장 두드러진 생략으로 남아있다. 여성들이 직물 산업에서 노동자로서 남성들을 훨씬 더 앞질렀지만 임금 지표나, 성장에 대한 토의나, 삶의 비용 기타 등등은 **오로지 남자들의 노동력에 대한 데이터만을 포함시킨다**.

이종현T의 Logical Point

여성 노동의 역할은 계속 생략되어있다는 내용의 반복이다. 따라서 빈칸에도 오로지 남성들만의 지표가 포함된다는 내용이 들어가게 되고 정답은 (C)가 된다.

40. 정답 : (C)

▶ 해석 : 법을 옹호해야 할 의무가 있지만, 판사는 자신의 재량권을 활용하여 일부 형벌의 잔혹함을 **경감**시켜줄 수 있다.

▶ 이종현T의 Logical Point

법을 지키는 것과 반대되는 의미가 필요하다. 따라서 법의 잔혹함에 대해서 인정해주지 않는다는 얘기가 되므로 정답은 (C)가 된다.

41. 정답 : (B)

▶ 해석 : 오늘날에도 영국에서 2,500여개의 기차역이 있어서 6백만 건 이상의 여행을 가능하게 해준다. 이렇게 많은 여행을 전산처리하는 것은 가능하지도 않고 또 **현명하지도** 않을 것이다. 그 가능한 여행들 중 상당수는 결코 행해지지 않는다. 예를 들어, 2007년에 Norfolk의 Buckenham 기차역에서 단지 10명만이 기차에 탔고, Cornwall의 Coombe Junction Halt 기차역에서 단지 15명만이 기차에서 내렸다는 것을 고려할 때, 혹 누구든 Buckenham에서 Coombe Junction Halt로 여행을 했을 **가능성은 매우 적다**. 비록 더 빠른 기차들이 이러한 여행을 좀 더 일반적인 것이 되도록 만들 수도 있겠지만, 이 두 장소 사이를 운행하는 기차들의 속도는 철도가 어떻게 운행되었는지를 이해하는 것과는 **관련이 없다**.

▶ 이종현T의 Logical Point

not A, nor B의 형태이다. A도 아니고 B도 아니라는 의미가 되므로 두 의미는 비슷한 내용이 들어가야 한다. 그리고 두번째 빈칸 앞 문장을 보면 기차역에서 매우 적은 인원이 탔으므로 가능성은 매우 적다는 내용이 들어간다. 그리고 세 번째 빈칸을 보면 부사절 내용이 속도가 여행을 흔하게 만들어줄 수 있을지라도 라고 되는데 그렇다면 주절은 반대가 들어가야 한다. 즉 흔하게 만들어주지 않는다는 내용이 필요하다. 따라서 정답은 (B)가 된다.

42. 정답 : (B)

▶ 해석 : 몇몇 역사학자들이 제왕적 대통력이라고 불렀던 쪽으로 향하는 경향은 20세기 초반에 시작되었다. 그 활동가인 루즈벨트 대통령 때문에, 그리고 그 대통령의 통치 하에서 **정점**에 도달했다. 그리고 그는 뉴 딜 정책을 계획하고 수행했다 의회로부터의 상당한 반대에도 불구하고.

▶ 이종현T의 Logical Point

시작을 한 이후의 결과에 대한 내용이므로 그 정점에 도달했다는 (B)가 정답이 된다.

43. 정답 : (A)

해석 : 자연의 관리를 위해 생태이론을 활용하려면 고층건물이나 로켓을 만들기 위해 물리이론을 활용하는 것과는 다른 규칙을 따를 필요가 있다. 엔지니어는 철강대들보 구조물을 만들 때의 응력이나 로켓에 적재된 것을 운반하기 위해 요구되는 추력에 대한 확고한 개념을 갖고 있는 반면, 생태학자는 그에 견줄 만한 개념을 갖고 있지 않다. 그런 경우에 생태이론이 통찰력을 이끌 수 있지만 그 통찰력은 문제의 생물들이 관련 모델의 가설에 얼마나 적합한지에 대한 그 지역 특유의 이해로 **조정되어야** 한다. 생태 관리자는 또한 어떤 개체군이 지속 가능한 수준으로 번식하도록 관리되거나 서로 다른 크기로 나누어진 서식지에서 유지되는 것이 이론상으로는 가능할지라도 보통은 개체군들이 워낙 소규모여서 존속이나 멸종이나 군체 형성에 관한 확고한 추정이, 따라서 예측이 **실행 불가능하다는** 점을 이해해야 한다. 만약 히말라야의 어떤 계곡에 세 마리의 눈 표범이 서식하고 있다면 이 고양잇과 동물들과 그들의 먹이를 관리하는 관리자는 그 지역 개체군이 사라지고 다른 개체들에 의해 대체될 수 있다는 점이나, 그 고양잇과 동물들이 다른 계속의 개체들과 서로 맞바꿔질 수 있다는 점을 이해할 때 도움을 받을 수 있다. 정량에 기초한 이동에 관한 실질적 추정능력은 실제로 확보 불가능할 가능성이 높다.

이종현T의 Logical Point

두번째 빈칸에서 개체들의 숫자가 너무 작다는 내용이므로 예측은 쉽지 않다는 내용이 들어가야 한다. 마찬가지로 첫번째 빈칸에도 정확하지 않다는 개념이 필요하다. 따라서 정답은 (A)가 된다.

44. 정답 : (D)

해석 : 시장에 대한 해석을 결정짓는 다양한 관점들을 통합하는 전체적 원리는 없지만, 폭넓은 분석적 접근법들 내에서 활용하기에 충분히 기민한 몇 가지 **발견적** 원리들이 있다.

이종현T의 Logical Point

부사절과 반대이므로 전체적 원리는 없다는 것의 반대로 전체적으로 될만한 것도 있다는 얘기가 필요하다. 그에 가장 부합할만한 선지가 (D)가 된다.

45. 정답 : (A)

해석 : 전설은 집단적 상상력 속에서 영구적으로 존속할 수 있으며 그것을 반증하고자 하는 반복된 시도에도 불구하고 놀라우리만치 **오래 지속**될 수 있다. 아틀란티스 전설이 그러한 생존자에 해당한다. 아틀란티스의 위치를 추측하는 수천 권의 저서가 써졌다. 이 모든 것은 아틀란티스라는 땅이 이전에 존재했다는 증거를 찾으려는 노력들이 실패했음에도 불구하고 쓰여진 것이다. 아틀란티스를 찾지 못한 것이 어느 누구의 노력이 부족해서도 아니다. 고고학자들, 지구 물리학자들 그리고 해양 탐험가들이 이 잃어버린 도시의 흔적을 찾고자 온갖 노력을 다해왔다. 이 주제를 광범위하게 다루어 온 어떤 작가는 아틀란티스에 대한 믿음이 여전히 가시지 않는 이유는 그것을 **부정**하는 증명을 하기 어렵다는 점이라고 말한 바 있다. 무엇인가가 결코 존재하지 않았다는 증거를 만들어낼 수는 없다.

이종현T의 Logical Point

in spite of 뒤의 얘기와 반대가 되므로 틀렸음을 입증하려 하지만 그게 안되고 계속 살아있다는 의미가 들어가야 한다. 그리고 두번째 빈칸에는 '빈칸'을 증명하기 어렵다고 했으므로 틀렸음을 증명하기가 어렵다는 이야기가 필요하다. 따라서 정답은 (A)가 된다.

46. 정답 : (D)

해석 : 그 영화평론가는 속편이 일반적으로 전편보다 못하다는 확신에 있어 **요지부동**이었지만, 그녀가 1편보다 뛰어나다고 여긴 '대부 2편'과 같은 예외를 가끔씩은 인정했다.

이종현T의 Logical Point

부사절과 주절은 반대이다. 주절에서 2편이 더 뛰어나다는 예외를 인정한다고 했으므로 부사절엔 인정하지 않는다는 내용이 필요하다. 따라서 정답은 (D)가 된다.

47. 정답 : (B)

해석 : 우리는 젊은이들에게 규칙과 법규를 지키게 해야 하지만, 이러한 규칙과 법규의 적용은 상식으로 **조절될** 필요가 있습니다.

이종현T의 Logical Point

법규를 지키게 해야한다는 것의 반대되는 것이므로 너무 지키게 할 필요는 없다는 얘기가 와야 한다. 따라서 정답은 (B)가 된다.

48. 정답 : (C)

해석 : 에밀리 브론테(Emily Bronte)의 소설 폭풍의 언덕(Wuthering Heights)에 관해 많은 평론가들은 소설의 후반부를 '낭만적인' 해석이 더 인정받고 있는 소설의 전반부를 뒤집지는 않더라도, 전반부에 대해 논평하면서 대조를 이루는 것으로 간주하고 있다. 서술자와 시간이동의 복잡한 활용에서 드러나는 정교한 소설구조가 이 소설의 두 부분을 전체로 이해하도록 부추긴다. 이러한 요소들이 이 소설 속에 있다는 것이 이 작가가 헨리 제임스(Henry James)에 견줄만한 소설적 구성에 대한 의식을 갖고 있다는 것을 반드시 입증하지는 않는다 하더라도, 이 요소들의 존재는 이 소설의 **다양한** 부분들을 통합하려고 시도하도록 부추긴다. 그러나 소설의 다양한 모든 요소를 통합하려고 시도하는 그 어떤 해석도 다소 설득력을 잃게 마련이다. 이는 폭풍의 언덕에는 부인할 수 없을 정도의 힘을 가진 다루기 힘든 여러 요소가 존재하며, 이 요소들이 결국, 모든 것을 통합하는 해석에 **포함**되기를 거부하기 때문이다.

이종현T의 Logical Point

첫번째 빈칸에 다양한 모든 요소를 통합하려고 나오므로 빈칸에도 같은 내용이 들어가야 한다. 그리고 두번째 빈칸에서는 반대되는 입장이므로 거부하는 것은 포함되는 것을 거부하는게 들어가야 한다. 따라서 정답은 (C)가 된다.

49. 정답 : (A)

해석 : **비굴한** 마을사람들은 그녀의 앞에서는 경의를 표했지만, 등 뒤에서는 그녀를 비웃었다.

이종현T의 Logical Point

등 뒤에서 그녀를 비웃었다는 내용과 반대되는 내용이므로 정답은 (A)가 된다.

50. 정답 : (C)

해석 : 마당, 공원, 정원 등에서 종종 발견되는 **독이 없는** 가터 뱀은 가끔 독사로 오인된다.

이종현T의 Logical Point

독이 있다고 오해된다고 나와 있으므로 반대되는 독이 없다는 말이 들어가야 한다. 따라서 정답은 (C)가 된다.

UNIT 3 시간을 이용한 대조

예 시 문 제

1. 정답 : (C)

해석 : 자연스럽게 발생된 천연두가 제거된 후에, 세계 건강 기구는 그것들이 나중에 다른 바이러스와 싸우는 수단으로 개발할 때 사용되어질 수 있다는 희망에서 그 바이러스의 남은 샘플들을 **보유하기로** 선택했다.

이종현T의 Logical Point

뒷 문장에 보면 나중에 사용되어진다고 나와있다. 그러므로 샘플을 계속 가지고 있다는 의미의 (C) retain이 정답이다.

2. 정답 : (E)

해석 : 19세기에 사이비 과학과 엉터리 약들의 인기는 사람들이 매우 **잘 속는다는** 것을 나타낸다. 그런데 오늘날 사람들이 잘 속는 것은 과거의 사람들이 냉철한 **회의론자**인 것처럼 보이게 한다.

이종현T의 Logical Point

첫번째 문장의 people과 두번째 문장의 citizens of yesterday는 같은 것이므로 묶어 준다. 그렇게 봤을 때 현대 사람들이 잘 속는 것을 보고 있으면 예전에 잘 속았던 과거의 사람들조차도 굉장히 냉철하고 잘 안 속는다는 의미가 되어야 하므로 정답은 (E)가 된다.

3. 정답 : (D)

해석 : 대중매체들은 한때 그 주지사가 전혀 무능하지 않다고 묘사했다. 그러나 그들은 이제 그녀를 **무능함**의 전형이라고 파악한다.

이종현T의 Logical Point

however로 역접이 되어 있으므로 빈칸에는 무능하다는 말이 필요하다. 따라서 정답은 (D)가 된다.

4. 정답 : (A)

해석 : 최근에 기억나는 그 어떤 것보다 이주민 문제가 유럽의 미래에 더 심각한 위협이 되고 있는데, 왜냐하면 그 문제는 중앙은행의 약속이나 다른 누군가의 현금 투입으로 해결될 수 있는 것이 아니기 때문이다. 이것은 유럽의 정체성에 대한 문제이고 그것(유럽의 정체성)이 한 세대 전에 유럽의 유권자들에게 가치 있었던 만큼 현재의 유권자들에게 가치 있는가에 관한 문제이다. **그러는 동안 내내** 난

민들은 계속 들어올 것이며, 그로 인해 유럽 정부들이 난민들을 받아들이는 희생을 하기는 더 어려워질 것이다.

이종현T의 Logical Point

이주민에 대한 문제를 계속 고민한다는 내용이 앞 내용이고 뒤에서는 난민들이 계속 들어온다고 되어 있으므로 고민하는 기간에도 계속 들어온다는 내용의 (A)가 정답이 된다.

5. 정답 : (D)

해석 : 반세기 전에, 의사들은 태아를 '완전한 기생자'로 생각했는데, 이는 태아가 자신이 필요한 것은 흡수하지만 자궁 안에서 어머니에게 해를 끼치는 모든 것으로부터는 스스로 봉쇄해버린다고 생각했기 때문이다. 미국 여성의 절반이 임신기간에 흡연을 했다. 아기들이 현재 태아 알코올 증후군으로 설명되는 장애를 지니고 태어났을 때에는, 그 원인을 **유전**으로 여겼다. 그때 이후로 임신기간 동안의 건강한 습관과 충분한 영양섭취는 아기가 조산이나 저체중 혹은 병을 갖고 태어날 가능성을 줄여준다는 것이 일반화되었다. 현재 많은 연구에서 태내 환경으로 인해 야기되는 문제들이 출생 시에는 드러나지 않지만 평생토록 영향을 미칠 수 있다는 사실을 보여주고 있다.

이종현T의 Logical Point

이 지문의 핵심은 Since then을 전후로 내용이 전환이 된다. Since then 이후의 내용은 임신했을 때 어떤 행동을 하는지가 중요하다는 것이고 앞 내용은 과거에는 상관 없다고 생각했다는 내용이다. 그리고 빈칸은 앞 부분과 관련이 있는 내용이 된다. 따라서 임신한 이후의 행동과 태아는 아무런 상관이 없다는 내용이 빈칸에 들어가야 한다. 그에 대한 정답은 (D)가 된다.

6. 정답 : (B)

해석 : 마틴 루터 킹 주니어(Martin Luther King Jr.)는 가장 뛰어난 연설가들 중 한 명이었는데, 그 이유가 언뜻 보기에는 분명한 것처럼 보인다. 그 젊은 목사는 학식을 갖추고 있었고 몹시 재능이 있었을 뿐 아니라 그 어떤 것도 **운에 맡기지 않았다**. 그가 한 웅변(연설)의 한 마디 한 마디는 모두 세심하게 준비된 것이었다. 이와는 대조적으로 준비를 하지 않은 것 같은 사람들의 운명을 생각해보라. 2012년 당시에 텍사스 주지사였던 릭 페리(Rick Perry)는 그해에 예정돼 있던 대통령 선거의 공화당 후보로 총애를 받고 있던 인물이었다. 토론에서 보여준 그의 언변은 **견디기 힘들** 정도였기 때문에 그의 당선 가능성은 줄어들었다. 한 토론에서 어떤 기자는 "릭 테리가 막 뇌졸중에 걸린 것 같다는 생각이 든다." 라고 트위터에 게시했다.

이종현T의 Logical Point

첫번째 빈칸에서는 마르틴 루터 킹은 준비된 사람이라고 나온다. 따라서 우연은 아니라는 내용인 chance가 들어가면 되고 뒤에 나오는 Rick Perry는 그 반대이다. 준비가 안되어 있으므로 토론은 못했다는 내용이 들어가야 한다. 따라서 정답은 (B)가 된다.

7. 정답 : (B)

해석 : Cartoon Art 박물관의 요새같은 정면은 방문객들에게 만화가 종종 **공격받는** 예술의 형태라고 상기시켜주도록 계산된 것 같다.

이종현T의 Logical Point

첫번째 문장에 박물관이 요새같다고 나와 있다. 따라서 빈칸에도 요새와 관련된 의미가 필요하고 그랬을 때 공격받는다는 (B)가 정답이 된다.

8. 정답 : (D)

해석 : 우리의 생물학적인 특별함은 물질의 효과가 **사람에 대한** 실험에 의해 증명되어져야만 한다고 요구한다. 심지어 그 물질의 효과에 대한 수천번의 테스트가 동물에 있은 후에도.

이종현T의 Logical Point

even after을 보며 대조되는 대상을 찾아준다. 여기서는 동물과 대조되는 대상을 찾으면 되므로 정답은 (D)가 된다.

9. 정답 : (A)

해석 : 과거에는 대중적인 중교집단들이 각자 **고립 상태로** 활동했다. 이제는 더 이상 그렇지 않다. 세계화의 영향이 포스트모더니즘의 영향과 병행하고 있으며, 어떤 면으로는 더욱 강화시키고 있다. 사상들이, 특히 종교적 견해들이, 확산되고 있는 상황에서 세계화 – 특히 전 세계 모든 지역으로의 커뮤니케이션의 확산의 영향 – 는 집단들이 더 이상 고립되어 있지 않다는 것을 의미한다. 전 세계적이면서 광범위한 변화로 인해, 종교는 점점 더 공적인 영역에서 밀려나 사적인 영역으로 들어가고 있다. 과거에는 종교적 전통에 **균열(분열)**이 발생하면, 그러한 분리가 원상태로 다시 회복되거나, 아니면 계속 독립적인(분리된)상태로 있을 경우 시간이 지나면 벗어나고 싶어 했던 다양성을 다시 반영하게 되었다. 이와는 대조적으로 오늘날에는 예를 들어 천주교가 신교의 카리스마적인 종교들에 자리를 내주고 있는 라틴 아메리카에서 천주교의 붕괴가 보여주고 있듯이 그러한 분열이 쉽게 억제되지 않는다.

이종현T의 Logical Point

첫번째 빈칸 아래에 보면 means that groups are no longer isolated가 나와 있고 더 이상 고립되지 않았다는 현재 얘기가 나와있다. 따라서 첫번째 빈칸의 과거는 반대 내용이 필요하고 첫번째 빈칸에는 고립되었다는 얘기가 필요하다. 그리고 두번째 빈칸 뒤쪽을 보면 마지막 부분에 오늘날 얘기가 나와 있고 그러한 분열은 쉽게 억제되지 않는다고 나와 있다. 따라서 그 문장 앞 부분 내용은 오늘날과 비교되는 과거 얘기가 되고 빈칸에는 분열이라는 의미가 들어가야 한다. 따라서 정답은 (A)가 된다.

10. 정답 : (C)

해석 : 초기의 연구들은 종종 대중들이 대중매체의 선동적인 영향에 **취약하다고** 결론지었다. 그러나 한 최근의 연구는 대조적으로 대중매체는 사회적인 태도와 행동에 있어서 거의 뚜렷한 화도 만들지 못한다고 나타낸다.

이종현T의 Logical Point

but 뒤의 문장에서는 대중매체가 대중들에게 영향을 주지 못한다고 나와 있으니 but 앞에는 반대되는 내용이 필요하다. 따라서 정답은 (C)가 된다.

11. 정답 : (E)

해석 : 자이언트 판다가 과거에는 중국의 넓은 지역에서 살고 있었지만, 지금은 **멸종**에 가까운 상태이다. 과거에 자이언트 판다는 중국 남부와 동부의 숲 전체에 퍼져 있었다. 각각의 판다는 넓은 면적의 숲과 많은 대나무를 필요로 했지만, 수만 마리의 자이언트 판다가 살기에 충분할 만큼의 숲과 대나무가 있었다. 하지만 20세기에 들어 사람들이 숲 속에서 들어와 대나무를 베어 버렸다. 1990년대 무렵, 과학자들은 야생 판다가 약 1,000마리밖에 남지 않은 것으로 추정했다. 다행스럽게도 중국 정부는 야생 판다를 구하기 위한 노력을 기울이기로 결정했으며, 판다 **보호구역**을 여러 곳에 만들었는데 이곳에서는 판다와 그들이 살고 있는 숲이 보호를 받았다.

이종현T의 Logical Point

빈칸 앞은 과거이고 빈칸이 있는 부분은 현재이므로 둘은 대조가 된다. 따라서 첫번째 빈칸에는 없어진다는 얘기가 필요하다. 그리고 두번째 빈칸에는 팬더가 없어지는 와중에 좋은 점이므로 팬더를 없애려고 하지 않는다는 내용이 필요하다. 따라서 정답은 (E)가 된다.

12. 정답 : (A)

해석 : 우리는 그때까지 가장 **재미없는** 연사였던 사람이 단 한 번의 연설로 청중들을 열광시키고 벌떡 일어나 환호하게 만들 수 있다는 사실에 어안이 벙벙해졌다.

이종현T의 Logical Point

대중들을 열광하게 해서 놀랐으므로 이때까지는 놀라게 할 능력이 없었던 사람으로 보여졌다는 얘기가 들어가야 한다. 따라서 정답은 (A)이다.

13. 정답 : (C)

해석 : 소설가 샬롯 스미스(Charlotte Smith)의 잉글랜드의 삶과 법률에 대한 명시적 암시적 비판은 1780년대에 시작됐는데 이것은 그녀에게 **"체제 전복적"**이라는 명성을 안겨주었다. 그녀의 소설들에는 잉글랜드의 법률 제도에 대한 최초의 문학적 비판들이 일부 담겨 있다. 이후에 등장하는 찰스 디킨스(Charles Dickens)와 같은 19세기 소설가들의 폭로기사들에 비하면 샬롯 스미스의 비판은 꽤나 소심한 편이다. 그러나 후대의 소설가들에게 그러한 대상을 소개한 이가 그녀였으며, 그녀가 그런 비판을 행하였을 때 그녀는 워낙 대범한 것으로 여겨져 **'위협'**이 되는 인물이라는 비난이 나올 정도였다는 것은 부인할 수 없는 사실이다.

이종현T의 Logical Point

비판과 관련된 표현이고 뒤에도 그런 내용이 있으므로 그와 관련된 단어가 들어가고 중간에 다른 것들에 비해선 약했지만 처음 이런 비판을 시작했다는 얘기가 있으므로 첫번째 빈칸과 비슷한 맥락의 이야기가 들어가야 한다. 따라서 정답은 (C)가 된다.

14. 정답 : (B)

해석 : 질병과 서식지 파괴로 매우 많은 수가 **죽었기** 때문에, 코알라는 지금 유칼리나무 숲 속의 아주 외진 곳에서만 찾아볼 수 있다.

이종현T의 Logical Point

아주 외진 곳에서만 찾아볼 수 있다는 것과 관련된 내용이 들어와야 한다. 따라서 정답은 (B)가 된다.

‖‖ 저자 소개 ‖‖

▌이 종 현

- 한양대학교 서울캠퍼스 경영학부 졸업
- (전) 지플랜어학원
- (전) 평촌 학원가 블라썸에듀 수능 대표강사
- (현) 아이브라운 인터넷 강의 독해영역 대표강사
- (현) 브라운편입학원 독해/논리영역 대표강사

이것이 논리다!

2021년 7월 5일 1판 2쇄 발행

저 자 이 종 현
발행인 남 승 우

발행처 도서출판 상尚 학學 당堂

서울특별시 동작구 사당로9가길 6
TEL : 02) 595-1692 ~ 4
FAX : 02) 595-1394
E-mail : shdbooks@naver.com
신고 : 2-155호 (1968. 11. 29)

정가 20,000원

ISBN 978-89-6587-199-6 03740